Truth, Prayer, Identity,

and the Spiritual Journey

Truth, Prayer, Identity, and the Spiritual Journey

James P. Danaher

Paragon House

First Edition 2019

Published in the United States by
Paragon House
Saint Paul, Minnesota

www.ParagonHouse.com

Bible references from the New Revised Standard Version unless otherwise noted.

Library of Congress Cataloging-in-Publication Data

Names: Danaher, James P., author.
Title: Truth, prayer, identity, and the spiritual journey / James P. Danaher.
Description: First [edition]. | St. Paul, Minnesota : Paragon House, 2019.
Identifiers: LCCN 2018051672 | ISBN 9781557789389 (pbk. : alk. paper)
Subjects: LCSH: Christian life. | Spiritual life--Christianity. |
   Truth--Religious aspects--Christianity. | Theology.
Classification: LCC BV4501.3 .D3595 2019 | DDC 230--dc23 LC record
available at https://lccn.loc.gov/2018051672

Manufactured in the United States of America

10 9 8 7 6 5 4 3 2 1

The paper used in this publication meets the minimum requirements of American National Standard for Information Sciences—Permanence of Paper for Printed Library Materials, ANSIZ39.48-1984.

Dedicated to the memory of my mother, who always,
like God, gave me permission and told me I could.

Acknowledgment

As always I would like to thank Willard K. Pottinger my proof-reader and reluctant editor whose insights and suggestions are always invaluable. Also my thanks to Gordon Anderson whose philosophical and theological insights have also shaped this final project into something much better than it would have been without his participation. I also want to thank Rosemary Yokoi who is always quick to insert words of encouragement that are always a blessing. Finally, I would like to thank Dorian Alu for her contribution and finishing touches to this effort.

Contents

Introduction

AS CHILDREN, WE LEARNED how the world worked, and we had little choice but to accept what we learned as true. Eventually, we became aware of other times and places where people believed that things worked differently. Just a few hundred years ago most people were unaware of such other times and places. The truth they received at their mother's knee was often the same truth they died believing. What human beings believe to be true in terms of knowledge, however, does change over time; but in the past, the changes happened so slowly that few people seemed to notice. Furthermore, without public education and travel, most people were unaware of the fact that our ideas concerning what was true were relative to a particular time and place. Not only have public education and travel made us aware of those who saw things differently from the way we see them today, but presently people who have lived a number of years know that what they learned about science and religion at earlier times in their life is not what they believe today. Many people find this terrifying and wish to retreat to an earlier age when they could imagine a more stable notion of truth.

Others embrace the changes but still naively imagine that at some point in the future we will arrive at a sustainable truth that does not have to change in order to accommodate the endless flow of new data that present anomalies to whatever our understanding happens to be. Of course, such a belief supposes that at some point in the future all the data will be in, and there will be no new data to present anomalies to the theories out of which we make sense of the world. People like Aristotle and Newton believed that we were close to such a point centuries ago. It is difficult to be so naïve today. What possibly could serve as evidence for having reached such a point? In the past, we believed some theories for hundreds or even thousands of years before new data revealed such truths to be the conventions of a particular time and place. How would we ever know if we were at a final understanding and there was no chance of future data making the truth of that understanding obsolete?

Certainly, there is local truth based upon the conventions of language and our present theories, but ultimately we discover data for which those theories cannot give an account, and we have to create perspectives and theories that can make sense of such data. From this point in our history, the best we can do in terms of knowledge is to operate out of the theories that make the most sense of the data that is available to us at this point in our history. Unlike people in the past who imagined that they were dealing with absolute truth in terms of knowledge, we can no longer be so naïve. Today, truth, as something to know, is no longer the absolute it appeared to be in the past.

There is, however, another notion of truth that is more than merely the object of knowledge. When Jesus says, "I am the way, and the truth, and the life,"[1] he is not speaking of truth as simply something to know but a way to *be*. Truth as something to *be* is very different from truth as merely something to know. For one thing, truth as something to be involves beauty and goodness in a way that truth as something to know does not. We do not generally

---

1.   John 14:6.

think of truth as something to be. Our common notion of truth more resembles that of Aristotle rather than Jesus. Aristotle had claimed that human beings were involved in the three basic activities of making, doing, and knowing. When we make, we want to make what is beautiful; when we do, we want to do what is good; and when we know, we want to know what is true. That notion of truth has shaped Western civilization, especially in the modern era. Science seeks a truth that is something to know, without concern for whether such truth is beautiful or good, but we are at a point in human history where we can see that such a truncated notion of truth does not have the absolute quality that many in time past imagined. Not only is such a truth narrow, in the sense of being something merely to know, but, as something to know, it is also relative to our perspectives that have to change in order to accommodate the constant flow of new data that is so much a part of our human condition and history. I remember an author recounting a story about when she was four years old and told her mother, "I think I now know everything I need to know." Her mother responded, "No, you don't," and the child replied, "I think I do." We never fully outgrow that sense that we now know all that we need to know. There is something attractive about a truncated notion of truth that we are able to possess. This is especially the case with spiritual truths.

Over the last two thousand years, most people who consider themselves Christians do so because of what they believe to be true about Christianity. A Christian is someone who believes Jesus was born of a virgin, died and rose from the dead, that he is the second person of the God-head, and whatever else the creeds of one's denomination insist that Christians believe. The truth of Christianity as something to know and believe rather than something to be is certainly attractive. The promise of eternal life for simply believing certain epistemic truths concerning Jesus' life and death is more appealing than a Christianity that calls us to an ontological truth of *being* like Jesus. This is especially true if we consider the actual teachings of Jesus, which if we are honest, make little sense to most people. Who really believes that it makes sense not to resist evil, to turn the other cheek, to give alms to all who ask, and to forgive all who sin against us, even to the point of loving our enemies?[2] Such teachings of Jesus are crazy, or at least they appear irrational from the perspective of everything we know about the world. Throughout the history of Christianity, there have been those who have taken Jesus' notion of truth as something to *be* seriously. In order to do so, however, they had to get to a different perspective from which they were able to see Jesus' words as divinely beautiful and supremely good, rather than simply crazy. That perspective has not changed over the last two thousand years. While what we claim to know about scientific and theological truth has altered enormously over the last two thousand years, the perspective that allows us to see the beauty and goodness of Jesus' words has not changed.

This book explores that perspective that allows us to see the beauty and goodness of Jesus' words. The mystics referred to that perspective as prayer, but their notion of prayer was very different from the way most people understand that term today. Most people understand prayer as some form of communication with

---

2. Matthew 5:39-44.

God, rather than a perspective or place from which we can see the beauty and goodness of Jesus' words.

From our normal place of being in the world, we have little choice but to ignore the words of Jesus, which seem to reflect a divine perspective rather than one appropriate for human beings. Popular forms of Christianity are quick to remind us that Jesus is Divine and because of that, his prescription for how to *be* is beyond us. Popular forms of Christianity often add that because the prescription Jesus offers is beyond us, God has made another way for us to gain eternal life merely by believing that Jesus paid for our sins and we have gained heaven on his merit rather than our own. That is certainly true but it can have the negative effect of causing us to pay little attention to Jesus' words, which we all too easily see as superfluous. Of course, that might be a reason for the popular gospel's appeal, since the teachings of Jesus are difficult and perhaps even impossible from a normal human perspective. Indeed, to see the beauty and goodness of Jesus' words we need the divine perspective to which Jesus calls us, and we only get to that perspective through a spiritual journey into the deepest recesses of our soul. The journey may begin in an instant but it is a life-long journey of descent into the mystery of who we are in God.

This journey has always been the objective of the mystic but today it is more common than ever since we have reached a point in human history where we find ourselves engulfed in mystery. Twenty-first century science is more mysterious than early modern science could have imagined. There seems to be no bottom to the microscopic world, and we just have to put our exploration on hold until we invent ever more-powerful instruments to explore the seemingly endless depth of the microscopic world. The same seems to be the case concerning the macrocosm of the universe, whose exploration requires ever more-powerful telescopes, but which never bring us to the end of what is out there. Likewise, we have encountered anomalies that we label dark matter and dark energy because they represent data for which our present scientific paradigm has no explanation.

We are always trying to make sense of our world and reduce it to what is knowable—to make it fit within our understanding—but the world refuses to cooperate. The same is true in the spiritual realm. We create religious doctrines that attempt to make sense of God and our relationship with God, but the words of Jesus are the perennial "dark matter" and "dark energy" that confound our attempts at truth in terms of something we can know. Instead, Jesus' words draw us into that deeper level of being that is prayer, where we can perceive the beauty and goodness of Jesus' truth. The spiritual journey of which Jesus and the mystics speak is not a journey into greater levels of knowing but deeper levels of awareness from which to perceive the mystery of God and our connection to that mystery. Discovering the truth of our being, however, is not like discovering the truth of an answer to a question. As we will see, Jesus seldom answers our questions but instead leads us on a spiritual journey to that deeper level of being in God rather than being in the world.

Spiritual journeys are not about religious beliefs. Religions and their beliefs tell us what we should believe about God and ourselves, while spiritual journeys lead us into experiencing God and ourselves at deeper, ineffable levels of awareness. Modern religions give us something to believe in, while spiritual journeys beckon us to a deeper way to *be*. Religions build up our confidence in what we know and believe, while spiritual journeys reduce that confidence and bring us to a deeper experience of both God and ourselves. In order for that to happen, however, we have to beginning by rethinking our cultural concepts of truth, prayer, and identity.

CHAPTER ONE

Truth

IN THE LATE MEDIEVAL WORLD, nearly everyone believed what Aristotle had explained about how the world worked, but with the advent of the microscope, we became aware of data of which Aristotle knew nothing. In order to account for the new data, many of the great thinkers of the seventeenth century, including Galileo Galilei, Rene Descartes, John Locke, Isaac Newton, and Robert Boyle (just to mention a few) developed a new understanding of the world that came to be known as the Corpuscular Philosophy. Eventually, this new way of seeing the world evolved into modern atomic chemistry. By the eighteenth century, Enlightenment philosophers and scientists thought that we were close to completing human knowledge and that ultimate truth was within our grasp. The advanced technology of subsequent centuries, however, has revealed an endless flow of new data that require new perspectives and paradigms in order to make sense of the new data.

Aristotle's understanding of the world has certainly become obsolete, but one aspect of Aristotle that many retain is his concept of truth because Aristotle's notion of truth is one we all receive as children. We all begin our human existence in a strange and unfamiliar world where we must depend upon others for our care. We have little or no idea of what is going on, but those who care for us seem to know and they begin to acculturate us into their understanding. It is essential to our social and psychological well-being that we accept this acculturation as true and even certain. Much of this acculturation comes through language acquisition; so it is natural for us to believe that the understanding we are acquiring through language mirrors the world in which we find ourselves. This is our earliest experience, and Aristotle gave us a way to confirm that experience.

Aristotle believed that the world was knowable and that language gives us access to that knowledge. Thus, by understanding the order we find in language, we can understand the order in nature itself. Since words, with the exception of pronouns and personal nouns do not designate individual things, but rather species or kinds of things, Aristotle reasoned that we must have some native ability to put individual things together into the natural groupings to which we assign words. In order for that to happen, the kinds of things words designate must share a similar form, and we must have an innate ability to identify those forms. What he claimed was that in addition to a passive intellect, which simply records sense data, we also possess an active or agent intellect that gives us the ability to pick out the actual forms that create the kinds of things that exist within nature.

Aristotle's thinking had an enormous effect upon Western thought, but that effect was late in coming. Although Aristotle was an ancient Greek (384-322 BC), Western Europe did not experience the full breadth of Aristotle's thinking until fifteen hundred years after his death. Aristotle's formal writings did not survive the ancient world, but Muslim scholars in the Middle East had preserved what amounted to his lecture notes. These works eventually found their way into Spain through the Moors, and eventually to several of the great learning centers in Europe. At first, the medieval church condemned the teachings of Aristotle, but Thomas Aquinas (1225-1274) at the University of Paris was able to interpret Aristotle in a way that the church found acceptable. With Thomas' canonization in 1323, Aristotle's view came to dominate the late medieval church and world.

The Christian Aristotelianism of the late medieval world allowed us to believe that knowledge was possible because God had equipped human beings with an active intellect by which we could know how to organize our language according to the order that God had built into the world. If our conceptual understanding of the world comes through a God-given active intellect, then language is the mirror of nature and our linguistic concepts represent the kinds of things that God created. Consequently, truth is simply a matter of whether our statements about the world are factual. There is no question of different perspectives since we all share the same God-given perspective.

In such a world, educated and uneducated people both had the same or very similar views. Of course, the uneducated will always believe what they experience from the perspective they received through language acquisition and acculturation, and Aristotle provided a philosophy that claimed that they were right to do so because human beings are equipped with the ability to organize our language according to the actual order within nature. Thus, in the late medieval world, both the uneducated and educated trusted that language mirrored nature.

Today, that is no longer the case and educated people often see things differently than the uneducated. Recent studies have revealed that twenty-five percent of Americans believe that the sun goes around the earth rather than the earth going around the sun. For the most part that was not the case in the late medieval world of Aristotle where nearly everyone believed that the sun went around the earth. Furthermore, even Christians and Muslims had very much the same perspective since it was the Moors who introduced Aristotle into Western Europe. Under the Moorish rule in Spain, Christians, Jews, and Muslims all lived and prospered together within the same society. The Moors were eventually defeated and pushed out of Spain in 1492, after which Christian Europeans took charge in Spain and expelled the Jews. If Aristotle was a factor that contributed to holding a diverse religious population together, the seventeenth century brought changes that meant the end of Aristotle and the end of the kind of metanarrative that Aristotle provided.

Several factors contributed to the end of Aristotelian thinking. The exploration of the Americas and other remote parts of the world in the 16th century revealed that the world was not only much bigger than Aristotle had imagined, but it was more diverse as well. As long as the medieval world was limited to Europe, it was easy to believe in an active intellect and the idea that we all experienced and understood the same world because of a God-given ability to perceive the world as God had created it. When our experience was limited to Western Europe, although different languages had different sound bites or names, those words generally designated the same or very similar concepts or kinds of things. When we discovered remote people who looked, dressed, and even conceptualized their experience into concepts or kinds of things differently than Europeans, the Aristotelian belief in an active intellect faced a challenge. Such differences meant one of two things. Either medieval Aristotelians were wrong about their

God-given understanding, and language's ability to mirror nature, or those remote people who had such different ways were not really of our species and did not enjoy the benefit of a God-given ability to have a correct understanding of the world, as Europeans did. When given a choice of either questioning our own understanding or inventing racism in order to preserve our own prejudices, we generally choose to preserve our prejudices. Thus, racism and the genocides that followed preserved our prejudice that we perceived and understood the world as God intended. Indeed, many people continue to maintain such beliefs in order to preserve their prejudices, but the other factor that challenged Aristotle's view of the world was more formidable.

At the end of the sixteenth and beginning of the seventeenth centuries, we invented the microscope (1590) and telescope (1608). Certainly, the telescope played a part in helping Galileo confirm Copernicus' claim of a heliocentric rather than a geocentric world, and that the universe was not as we initially imagined. It was the microscope, however, that led to the end of Aristotle's idea that language mirrored nature because of Aristotelian forms and our active intellect's ability to detect those forms. The microscope revealed a world unknown to Aristotle or anyone else. Suddenly, there was a world for which there was no inherited nomenclature and God-given understanding. If God had given us a natural ability to organize the world of nature, it stopped at the microscopic level. To complicate matters, a group of some of the most important seventeenth-century thinkers began to speculate that perhaps things were of a specific nature or kind, not because of Aristotelian forms, but because of the arrangement and motion of things that existed on the microscopic level.

It was some time before we created the concepts of atoms, molecules, subatomic particles, bacteria, viruses, and DNA in order to make sense of the microscopic world and the effect it had upon our everyday lives, but it all began in the seventeenth century with a new perspective dubbed the corpuscular philosophy or corpuscular hypothesis. Thinkers who left Aristotle in favor of the corpuscular philosophy included such notables as Galileo Galilei (1564-1642), Rene Descartes (1596-1650), Robert Boyle (1627-1691), John Locke (1632-1704), and Isaac Newton (1643-1727).

These corpuscularians made the first attempts at creating a new way of seeing the world and a new way of thinking about truth itself. What was so unique about these corpuscularians was the fact they were without a language and nomenclature to describe what they were experiencing on the microscopic level. By contrast, Aristotle had inherited a language and nomenclature that he believed mirrored nature, at least above the microscopic level. On the microscopic level, however, there were no ready-made words to describe what we were seeing on this new level of experience. Of course, we did have some words that were appropriate. We realized that things on that level of experience had characteristics like shape and extension, that we could number the things we observed there, and that they either moved or did not move. In time, these became the new primary qualities, which replaced Aristotle's primary qualities of earth, air, fire, and water, but these new primary qualities were the primary qualities of what? What was it that we were observing on this microscope level? The term and concept that these seventeenth-century thinkers settled on was *matter*, but that was just a term or sound bite without much meaning. Aristotle had used the term "matter" simply to individuate members of the same species or form, but never really told us what matter was. The Corpuscularians used the same term to identify what they were experiencing on the microscopic level. Their idea of matter, however, was not what individuated members of a specific form, as it did for Aristotle, but was rather the very stuff that created the form or species. Corpuscularians argued that it was the arrangement and motion of these material corpuscles (later dubbed atoms) on the microscopic level that produced everything we experience in our everyday lives. If the microscopic matter was the basis for everything that we experience, then it, rather than Aristotle's idea of substantial forms, was the cause of things being of one kind or another. If that were true, then Aristotle's idea of substantial forms was an illusion and so was his idea of an active intellect to detect such forms.

Consequently, the modern period began with two very different perspectives concerning the natural world, both claiming to be true. The truth of whether the Aristotelians or the Corpuscularians were right concerning the origin of natural kinds cannot be determined in the same way we determine the truth of facts since we are dealing not with facts but with the philosophical problem of how we should conceptualize and think about the world. What determines the truth of a perspective, or way of thinking about the world, is whether it can give an account and make sense of what we are experiencing. We often refer to this as "saving the appearance." Aristotle had certainly offered a perspective that made sense of his world, but it had nothing to say about the world that the microscope revealed. Historically, our perspectives change as new data baffles our old ways of making sense of the world and require us to come up with new ways of thinking about our experience.

We had seen such situations arise in the past where new experiences forced us to change the way we conceptualized and thought about the world, but never anything on this kind of scale. The microscope presented an unprecedented task for human beings. Aristotle had an inherited language, and only had to explain why it mirrored nature, but the corpuscularians were without an inherited language and consequently without an active intellect to tell them how to divide-up the microscopic world.

Thus, the Corpuscularians were on their own to create an order on the microscopic level, and they had to come up with a new theory about truth itself. With Aristotle, the truth was simply a matter of correspondence. A statement was true if it corresponded to observable reality. There was no question of the truth of a perspective since the medieval Aristotelians believed that our perspective or way of conceptualizing the world was God-given, rather than merely based upon the conventions of language. The corpuscular philosophy undermined that view since God had not given us an understanding of the microscopic world, which corpuscularians believed established the actual kinds of things we find in nature. Consequently, we were on our own without a language or active intellect to aid us in creating a new perspective or way of organizing our understanding of the world. If our perspective was no longer God-given but based upon the conventions of language, what could be the criterion for the truth of such a perspective?

For Aristotle, a correspondence theory of truth that either verifies or falsifies propositions based upon whether they correspond to observable reality worked fine, because how we conceptualized the world was a given. When that is no longer the case and we are on our own to decide how to conceptualize the world, correspondence will no longer do, since our ideas of how to conceptualize the world is no longer a given. Thus, what arose in the modern period was the idea that a theory or way of seeing the world could be considered true if it "saved the appearance" or made coherent sense of what we were experiencing. Coherence theories of truth are probably as old as philosophy itself, but coherent theories of truth became eminently pertinent in the modern period due to the microscope and all the speculation that followed from that.

Some historians trace the origin of the modern coherence theory of truth to Descartes who used mathematics and geometry for his idea of truth as coherence. Mathematics and geometry are true not because they correspond to observable reality but because they are internally consistent or coherent. Numerals and geometric figures are abstract ideas with immutable definitions or forms, which Descartes thought made mathematics and geometry the perfect examples of truth as coherence. If we are going to have to construct our own conceptualization of the world, Descartes thought that we should strive to make our theories coherent.

Of course, coherence theories, when they are about actual physical states of affairs rather than the purely abstract realm of mathematics and geometry, also have to *save the appearance*, or give an account of what we actually experience. At first, this did not seem to be enough to establish a belief as *true*, but as our understanding of the human condition progressed, it became ever more apparent that that might be the best we could achieve. Initially, late medieval or early modern thinking did not see coherence as a way to truth but merely a way to save the appearance. When Galileo started teaching Copernicus's theory of a heliocentric rather than geocentric universe, the church told him he could teach it as *saving the appearance* but not as truth, since Ptolemy's theory of a geocentric universe also saved the appearance or explained what we were seeing. The church thought that truth had to be more than merely some way to make sense of what we were seeing since multiple theories could do that. Galileo thought that Copernicus saved the appearance much better than Ptolemy did, and for that reason, we should consider Copernicus's theory true rather than Ptolemy's theory. In time, we came to recognize the coherence theory of truth as legitimate, although what always plagues the idea of coherence is the fact that multiple theories can save the appearance or make coherent sense of what we are experiencing. Several years ago, two economists with conflicting theories split the Nobel Prize for economics. Both theories were coherent and saved the appearance but could they both be true? Are there possibly multiple ways to make sense of the same data? Perhaps the greatest example of this problem with coherence is in theology where people read the same sacred text and come up with innumerable coherent theories concerning the truth and meaning of that text.

Coherence may not get us to an ideal notion of truth, but given what we now know concerning our human condition, it is often the best we can do. Not only is it essential when trying to determine the truth of a perspective or theory, but we even use coherence at times to determine the truth of facts. We employ it constantly in order to judge whether someone is lying. If we cannot get at the facts to either verify or falsify their story, rather than concede and claim we have no way of knowing whether their account is true or not, we make judgments based upon how coherent their story is. Certainly, if we are able to verify or falsify the details of the story by observation, or reproduce the details in an experiment, we would do that, but often we do not have access to the experience nor can we reproduce it, and thus must rely on how coherent the story is. This is often the case in courts of law. In such cases, we rely on the testimony of people and judge the truth of their testimonies on a basis of how coherent and consistent they are with what we know about human nature, the nature of the world, and the character of the person giving the testimony. Of course, the fact that one account appears more coherent than another does not mean that one is true and the other not true. It could simply be that one person explains or presents their theory better, and we deem the one theory true and the other false not on the merits of the facts but on the skill of the one who presents the more coherent explanation. This is often the case in debates and courts of law.

The biggest problem with coherence theories is that they are relative to history. Many theories appear coherent until new data appears for which those theories are unable to give an account. Throughout our history, we have created ways of making sense of our experience and treat those explanations as true until anomalies appear, and then we set out to find new perspectives and theories that can create a more coherent picture that better accounts for the new data. This is what is behind much of the history of civilization and what has caused our modern understanding to evolve into something very different from that of our ancestors. We even experience this in our own individual lives as new data often does violence to our understanding and forces us to think about things differently. This is especially true today where our ever-increasing technology presents us with data that requires us to adapt our understanding of that data.

In addition to our ever-expanding technology, contemporary zoological research continually reveals that human beings experience only a sliver of what really is out there. In the cartoons, Wile E. Coyote experiences the same world we do, but in reality, other animal species are equipped to experience a world of which we are oblivious. We may concede that other animal species have different ways of perceiving the world, but we naïvely imagine we are all perceiving the same world. That is a bit of metaphysics that is hard to defend today. Is there really one, objective world that is independent of the vast variety of perspectives and sense data that an unfathomable amount of animal and even plant species experience?

Whatever the case, the wisdom we derive by having arrived at a twenty-first century understanding of the human condition is that truth in terms of absolute knowledge is forever beyond our grasp. Our understanding will always be dependent upon a perspective that is the product of our imaginations' ability to make sense of the data before us. Our early modern ancestors may have imagined that we would eventually figure it all out, but that ambition has faded over the last two centuries. We simply continue to discover more and more data about the world and much of that data maligns whatever our present understanding happens to be. Furthermore, there is no reason to believe that at some point in the future there will be no new data to threaten whatever our understanding currently is.

In light of this, it should not be surprising that a third theory of truth has become popular. A little over a hundred years ago, two Harvard professors, Charles Sanders Peirce (1839-1914) and William James (1842-1910) suggested that perhaps it is better to think about what we take to be true by considering the consequences of a truth claim. In other words, ideas or propositions that are fruitful we should consider true and those that are not fruitful we should consider not true. Thinking of truth in terms of consequences or fruitfulness rather than facticity (correspondence) or "saving the appearance" (coherence) at first seems strange since up until the advent of pragmatism, truth was something that we considered as being impersonal and objective. Pragmatism introduced the idea that truth was more personal than we had previously imagined. William James argued that the only question that should matter concerning truth is what difference does it make whether one perspective or another is true? If it does not matter, why are we concerned with it? Truth is a matter of personal concern and trivial matters should not receive consideration as being true. To reduce truth to facticity (correspondence) or clarity (coherence) is often to trivialize truth.

James tells an interesting story to illustrate this point. He had been on a camping trip with some friends and upon returning from a hike, there was a discussion underway concerning a certain squirrel. Several campers had seen a squirrel place itself behind a tree so the campers could not see it. When the campers moved to one side of the tree to see the squirrel, the squirrel moved to keep the tree between itself and the campers. The campers continued to move around the tree and so did the squirrel. When the campers had circumnavigated the tree, the question arose whether they had gone around the squirrel. Some said yes, since they had circumnavigated the tree and likewise the squirrel, but others said no since they had not lapped the squirrel and the squirrel had always stayed ahead of them. We can take two things from this story:

First, our understanding is always relative to how we conceptualize something. The second thing, and James' main point, is what difference does it make if this or that particular understanding is true? This is not a question of truth but idle curiosity. For James, truth has to be more meaningful, and that meaningfulness is what is often missing with both correspondence and coherence theories of truth. Both correspondence and coherence speak of truth objectively as something to which we simply conform rather than something in which we participate. If it sounds strange to speak of truth as something we participate in, that is because we have learned to think of truth as something outside and independent of ourselves—something that we wish to know rather than something in which we take an active part. Such a notion of truth can give us a certain sense of security in believing that truth is something absolute or ultimately real in the sense of it being something beyond us but at the same time something we can connect to through knowledge. This is the notion of truth that we inherit from our science, religion, and philosophy. Pragmatism, however, moved away from that notion of objective truth and toward a more meaningful and personal notion of truth.

Shortly before Pierce and James began thinking about truth from a pragmatic perspective, the Danish philosopher Soren Kierkegaard (1813-1855) had also begun speaking of truth in a more personal way. Kierkegaard had personal religious experiences that did not mesh with his inherited theological understanding, which forced him to either dismiss his individual experiences as delusional or create an understanding of truth that could account for and makes sense of those experiences. This is the circumstance of the existential crisis. Of course, most do not take the existential option but instead dismiss the experiences that do not conform to our inherited understanding in order to maintain that conventional understanding and the security that comes with believing what everyone else believes. Some, however, take the existential option and set out on their own in the hope of finding a personally meaningful truth.

In the twentieth century, Martin Heidegger (1889-1976) continued that existential tradition and spoke of truth as something to *be* rather than simply something to know. Heidegger claimed that truth, as something to be, was the original quest of philosophy that predated Aristotle and the idea of truth as merely something to know. People who have not been trained in Western philosophy often suppose that philosophy is about finding the meaning of life, and they may be closer to the truth than those schooled in Aristotle and the epistemic tradition of truth as merely something to know.

Like Kierkegaard, Heidegger thought that truth had to be authentic and more meaningful to the individual than merely knowing and believing the conventional understanding of the world at a particular time and place in human history. Once we begin to think of truth as something to *be* rather than merely something to *know,* truth is no longer something out there in the world, but something deeply personal.

Ontological truth is the quest for meaning in our lives. Epistemic truth may provide the illusion of certainty in that it gives us a pseudo confidence in the belief that we know how things work but it does not answer our greatest question about the meaning of life. Many argue that there is no apparent meaning to life, but throughout our long history, some have gone on spiritual journeys in search of such truth. There is a long tradition of such interior journeys after truth and the meaning of life, especially in the East. The West also had its ancient and medieval mystics, but throughout most of Western history, the exploration of the interior world was not encouraged by Western religious institutions that tried to unite people through common sets of epistemic beliefs. In order to maintain the illusion that their beliefs represented spiritual truth itself, the Christian church historically dealt severely with heretics, sometimes by burning them alive.

Today, we know that epistemic truth is always local and dependent upon the conventional concepts and theoretical understanding of a particular time and place in human history. As more and more people become aware of this fact, many are beginning to opt for spiritual journeys that lead them into the kind of experience and way of being that has always been the truth to which Jesus has called us. Spiritual truth is not something to know and believe but something to experience and become. Spiritual truth is different from the kind of truth of which Aristotle, Descartes, or even William James spoke. The truth that a spiritual journey pursues much more resembles the truth of which Jesus speaks when he says, "I am the way, and the truth, and the life."[1] He is speaking of a truth that is a way to *be* and not something merely to know and believe. As a way to be, Jesus' truth is not merely true but divinely beautiful and good as well. You can be obedient to God by believing in the truth of God, but you can only fall in love with God by seeing how divinely beautiful and good God is. The truth that Jesus reveals is not something to know and

---

1. John 14:6.

believe but something to fall in love with and become because it is divine, beautiful, and good.

CHAPTER TWO

Personal Truth

WE ALL BEGIN BY IDENTIFYING with a particular cultural and historical group that gives us our inherited understanding of the world. Such an inherited understanding provides children with stable beliefs and values essential for their psychological and social well-being. It also provides a basis from which to build a sense of personal identity based on how well we manage to achieve the values of that culture. In contemporary America, those dominant values include wealth, power, and fame. Those who achieve such values establish a sense of personal identity above others. Wealth seems to be at the top of the list, since, in a capitalist society, money is not only a means of exchange and a store of value (capital), but it is also a measure of value. Just as we measure distance in miles and weight in pounds, we measure value in dollars. Many people see their worth as a human being in terms of money.

Likewise, power and fame are not very far behind wealth as possible bases upon which to build a personal truth and identity. What wealth, power, and fame have in common is that they establish an identity based on what other people think is valuable and our ability to achieve those valued ends. Furthermore, such an identity is quantitative. We measure our personal identity against others who have more or less wealth, power, or prestige than ourselves. If we lack the ability to acquire wealth, power, or fame, we generally look to other cultural values that are more achievable such as family, good friends, or satisfying and meaningful work. If we are not even good at those things, we might look to hobbies, criminal activity, or drug addiction as possible sources of identity.

Today, many people experience existential crises not because their understanding of the world and their place in it is destroyed by cataclysmic events like wars, famines, and natural disasters, but simply through education, which reveals how relative our world and our identification with it is to a particular time and place rather than to something enduring. Without an education, the world into which we have been oriented can look substantial, but education destroys that illusion. Once we understand the vicissitudes of history and the way that the human condition has changed over time to accommodate those changes, the identity that the world has imposed upon us no longer looks as substantial as it did when we were children and had little choice but to accept the world and the identity it imposed upon us. Today, perhaps more than ever before, many people sense that there is something wrong with how the world has identified them and they set out to find a deeper personal truth.

The rise and current popularity of psychotherapy is an example of people dissatisfied with who they have become and are in search of the factors that have contributed to that becoming. The exploration and discovery of suppressed wounds in childhood can help us to understand how the world has shaped the personal truth of our identity beneath our notice. By bringing such painful wounds to a conscious level, we are able to deal with them and reshape the personal truth of our being. Understanding suppressed wounds from childhood can be revealing concerning why we are the way we are, but it does not get us to the ultimate truth of who we are.

Most psychologists believe that another aspect that makes up a big part of who we are involves feelings and that part of getting at the personal truth of who we are is a matter of being in touch with those feelings, rather than suppressing them in order to more easily negotiate social interactions. What makes exploring those feelings so difficult is that our initial orientation to the world was largely about learning what feelings needed to be suppressed and what feelings were socially appropriate and acceptable. Thus, in trying to get at our deepest feelings, it is hard to know what feelings society has shaped, and what feelings are native to the personal truth of who we are. The easiest place to see this is regarding our sexual feelings. Our sexual feelings are both some of our strongest feelings and at the same time those that are often most suppressed by religion and other social institutions. Perhaps our deepest personal truth and identity has something to do with our authentic sexual feelings and gender orientation. We see this today with the rise of the LGBT community, who see their feelings toward sexuality and gender as essential to the truth of who they are as a person.

Other people understand their sexual feelings in a very different way. They do not consider their sexual feelings as part of one's personal truth and identity, but rather as sin unless expressed in very specific ways. Sex, when seen as sin, is not something we explore in order to come to a deeper personal truth, but something to avoid in all but certain socially prescribed ways. Many religious people believe that God provides such prescriptions for proper sexual behavior and that variation from such prescriptions is sinful. Sexual feelings can certainly be frightening even for those who do not see them as sinful, and it makes sense to place restrictions on those feelings for our own well-being and the well-being of others. To believe that God strictly prescribes those restrictions however is to imagine a rather parochial notion of God, and to ignore the biblical history where sexual norms do seem to change over time. Adultery today is a matter of having sex with someone who is not your wife or husband, but Jacob seemed to have no trouble having sex with, and producing children by, Rachel and her sister Leah, as well as two concubines. The twelve tribes of ancient Israel come out of one man and four women.

Sex is certainly a strange and mysterious part of our human condition but because we do not understand it, many of us want simply to avoid it by labeling it sinful and dismissing it from consideration as part of what contributes to the personal truth of who we are. For many people, sex is not only sinful but one of our most grievous sins.

In order to see how out of proportion our attitudes toward sex are, consider the following as a thought experiment. The Bible tells us that King David was a man after God's own heart, even though he was an adulterer with Bathsheba, a murderer with Uriah, and had a homosexual relationship with Jonathan. Many religious types have no problem with David being a Godly man in spite of his committing adultery and murder but react strongly to the suggestion that David's love for Jonathan was erotic or homosexual. Of course, we do not know if it was. What is interesting, however, is why many religious people react so strongly to such a suggestion. Is it because our sexuality involves some deeper, unconsciousness level of who we are? Adultery and murder are behavioral, but our sexual appetites involve something deeper and many prefer to stay on the surface of our existence and get our personal truth by identifying with tribal norms rather than exploring the truth of who we personally are on some deeper level.

Along with our ideas and feelings concerning sexuality, which are both deeply personal and culturally relative at the same time, our ideas of beauty and goodness are likewise both culturally imposed and deeply personal at the same time. We all begin with cultural or tribal notions of beauty and goodness. Our inherited notions of beauty and goodness vary over time and from culture to culture, but many people erroneously believe they are God-given. Of course, if we believe that, we have a basis for racism and all sorts of other cultural prejudices when we encounter people with different notions of beauty and goodness from our own. If we believe that our notions of beauty and goodness are God-given rather than a cultural inheritance that changes over time, we can easily believe that God has favored us when we encounter people with different notions of beauty and goodness. The modern racism that began five hundred years ago when Europeans began to encounter people from remote parts of the world was largely in response to how differently such people's cultural customs and dress were in comparison to Europeans. If God had given us our notions of beauty and goodness, such people were not as blessed as Europeans were. The immediate alternative to such racism seems to be a cultural relativism that is equally unsettling. The third option is to find a deeper basis for beauty, goodness, and truth than what we inherit from our culture but still share with other human beings with different cultural backgrounds. This was the project of Immanuel Kant (1724-1804).

Kant found the work of David Hume (1711-1776) unsettling. The empiricist Hume believed that all true ideas come out of experience, and if we cannot trace certain ideas back to an experience, it means they were the product of human imagination or sentiments of the heart. This was out of step with the rational thinking of the Enlightenment, and Kant set out to provide what he considered a more rational basis for such things than the imagination and affective sentiments that Hume had suggested. Kant argued that in order for us to have the kind of ideas that we have concerning truth, beauty, and goodness, there must be some innate mental hardware that allowed such ideas to arise from our experience. Instead of arguing that these ideas were either innate or merely the product of human imagination at work within culture and history, Kant argued that what was innate were the conditions that allowed such ideas to arise. Thus, although we know the world in which we find ourselves through experience, there must be certain innate conditions within us that allow for those experiences. In other words, although we often have conflicting ideas of what is true, beautiful, or good, there must be present within us certain universal conditions that allow us to make judgments concerning such things in the first place. Thus, at our core, Kant believed we all share a common, rational nature that allows us to think about things like truth, beauty, and goodness. Consequently, our human experience is not simply a result of experience, but a composite of experience and what we bring to the experience. Kant thought that what we brought to the experience were these innate conditions for all human experience. The next two centuries, however, revealed that what we brought to our experience was much more than just an innate mental hardware. The advent of historicism, the social sciences, and modern linguistics throughout the nineteenth and twentieth centuries revealed that in addition to whatever native hardware filtered our experience, the final product concerning what we think was also greatly shaped but historical, cultural, and linguistic factors.

Still, Kant's great contribution was to show us that our knowledge was something much more than the recording of experience. Furthermore, Kant maintained that we could reason about the native hardware that allowed for our uniquely human experience but it could never be known since he maintained that Hume was correct in assuming that all knowledge came through experience. Thus, whatever the conditions that allowed for human experience, like consciousness itself, we could never actually know since those conditions preceded and made knowing possible.

Kant was able to speculate and reason back from our actual experience to what must have been the conditions for such experience. In order for us to know the truth of the physical world in which we find ourselves, he reasoned that we must have innate ideas of things like time and space in order to organize our experience both in terms of memory (time) and concerning our external experience of the world (space). Likewise, in addition to thinking about what is true, we have some native ability to think about what is good beyond what our appetites and our specific culture tell us. Indeed, human beings do seem to have a moral compass that is able to take us beyond what both our appetites and culture tell us is good and Kant wanted to explore what that could possibly be. Since we do on occasion see individuals pursue a notion of goodness that is not the apparent result of appetite or custom, what makes someone do something that was not in the interest of either

themselves or their culture. Kant argued that there must be something deeper within us than our individual appetites or our conformity to culture, since some individuals are able to act according to
neither of those factors but instead pursue a notion of goodness that
is in everyone's interest. Kant argued that, when we do that, we are
acting according to that deeper rational nature and thus the ultimate
notion of goodness that we share with all human beings.

In the twentieth century, John Rawls (1921-2002) suggested
a way to get at a deeper and more universal truth than the ones
we concoct in order to accommodate our appetites and cultural
prejudices. In his now-famous book, *A Theory of Justice*, Rawls
employs the imagination in order to get us beneath the prejudices
of self-interest that keep us from seeing what real justice looks
like. Our idea of justice, like our ideas of truth, beauty, and goodness, is usually relative to our own self-interest. Consequently,
when people find themselves in positions of power in a given
society, they construct justice in their own interests. This is the
argument that Thrasymachus puts forth against Socrates in Plato's
Republic; justice is whatever the powerful say justice is. It takes
Socrates the ten books of the Republic to refute that idea by claiming that justice is to the soul what health is to the body. Of course,
that leaves us with the question of what health to the soul looks
like, other than the answer that it would look like Socrates.

Rawls does not attempt to tell us what justice ultimately is
but he does suggest that we could come up with principles upon
which to create a just state that everyone would agree to if we
made those decisions from behind a veil of ignorance where we
knew nothing about ourselves. As long as we know our gender,
race, educational level, economic status, age, religion, etc., we

create a concept of justice that is in the interest of those factors. What Rawls suggests is that if we knew none of those things, we would opt for very different principles that would benefit us if we found ourselves being one of the least privileged members of society. One of the first principles that we would create from such a perspective would be the idea of equal access. Not knowing anything about ourselves, we would not know if we were privileged members of society or marginalized members. Thus, to protect ourselves from the possibility of being a marginalized member of society because of our race, gender, age, or disability, we would opt for a society where everyone had equal access to the basic needs of things like food, shelter, medicine, and education. Rawls goes on to explain other aspects of the principles that we would create from beyond this imaginary veil of ignorance including principles such as *noblesse oblige* and that we should distribute wealth in the best interest of society.

Of course, if it turns out that someone was a privileged member of society, that privilege would be limited by the principle of *noblesse oblige* or, as Jesus says, "to whom much has been given, much will be required."[1] Rawls, however, argues that it would be a small price to pay rather than finding oneself a marginalized member of society without access to basic needs. Thus, the idea of justice constructed from behind a veil of ignorance would look very different from justice as it actually exists in the world. What happens in the real world is very different in that once we know who we are and what our station in life is, we opt out of self-interest, and people in positions of power create our ideas of justice in

---

1. Luke 12:48.

their interests and impose those ideas upon the rest of us. That is the nature of the real world and it is very different from the world we would create from behind a veil of ignorance.

Interestingly, the imaginary world of Rawls is very real to some people. Indeed, it is the world of the mystic, whose meditation or contemplative prayer takes them to a place that transcends all the concerns and distractions that make up our life and identity in the world. In prayer or meditation, the mystic goes beneath their sexuality and beneath the childhood wounds that contribute to the make-up of our personalities, and they descend to the level of pure consciousness that is beyond our appetites and cultural prejudices. In our normal mode of consciousness, we focus our minds upon an endless stream of thoughts that constantly occupy our attention. The mystics' prayer, however, is that altered state of consciousness, which refuses to acknowledge that endless flow and focuses instead upon the very consciousness that usually goes unnoticed because we are so preoccupied with all the thoughts that demand our attention.

In our normal state, our awareness focuses either upon the world that surrounds us or interior thoughts concerning our interaction with the external world. In prayer or meditation, all particular thoughts are absent and the mystic experiences the silence of consciousness itself. The mystic believes this is the deepest level of our being and the place at which we can become aware of our connection to the Divine. It is our soul, which God has created in the Divine likeness. This is where we began our lives as pure consciousness without any content. Of course, our orientation to the world demanded that we focus that consciousness upon the world that surrounds us and compels us to interact with it. The mystic's prayer is a retreat from that interaction. Furthermore, as we spend time with God in that deepest recess of our soul, we begin to take on an identity in God from which we can see the lie of the identity we had created for ourselves in the world.

For most people prayer is something they do out of their normal state of consciousness where they focus their attention upon God and communicate both their thankfulness and desires to God. The mystic's prayer is considerably different in that while most pray by focusing their attention on God and then making petitions to that God, the mystic sees God as a mystery that exceeds our understanding, but we can experience that God in the silence of pure consciousness. Many people have never experienced pure consciousness, since in our normal state of mind consciousness is what makes us aware of everything else. We seldom take the time and make the effort to enter that peaceful state of prayer that focuses upon the soul at rest.

We do not easily achieve this state of prayer where we transcend the clutter that usually occupies our attention. Our initial attempts to do so generally last but a few seconds. We find our minds constantly occupied with thoughts and feelings over which we have little control. Being able to experience pure consciousness, where we force our attention upon nothing but consciousness itself is difficult. Stopping the constant flow of thoughts that fill our minds and keep us from the great silence at the core of our being is not easy. It certainly requires a practice, but the process is quite simple. Indeed, it has not varied over the thousands of years that people have practiced meditation or contemplative prayer in a vast variety of cultures. Essentially, the process is one of stopping the endless flow of thoughts that flood our minds and that keep us from the peace that comes from pure, uncluttered consciousness.

In our normal state of mind, we find ourselves thinking something and then wondering why that particular thought has come to mind. Seconds later, another thought crosses our mind and we begin to think about that. In order to take control of our mind, meditation or deep prayer is a way of stopping this endless and undirected flow of thought and experiencing a certain peace that comes from that stillness. In order to get to such a place, some use a mantra and constantly repeat a word or phrase, thereby preventing any other thoughts but the mantra to enter their consciousness. Others simply let those ideas that come to mind pass without attaching our attention to them until all ideas have passed and only consciousness remains. This can provide a certain rest for a mind wearied by a constant flow of thoughts, but many of the great mystics claim there is more to this experience and when our gaze is turned inward upon consciousness itself, we experience more than a great silence that produces a state of peace.

The mystic's claim is that the great silence they experience in prayer is the ineffable experience of the Divine, but it is quite different from what most religious types consider prayer. Prayer to most religious people is focusing their attention upon God. What that really means is that they focus their attention upon their idea of God. Devoutly religious people will insist it is not their idea of God but God himself that they focus upon. By contrast, the mystic experiences God as a great mystery that exceeds our understanding and therefore silence is closer to the reality of God rather than whatever ideas of the Divine we might muster. For the mystic, the best that we can do in prayer is to clear a space from which we can be still before God. For the mystic, prayer is that ineffable experience of the great silence of God's presence, and the way that it silences us by experiencing it. This is what the psalmist understood when he wrote, "Be still and know that I am God."[2] In the stillness of God's presence, we are beneath the level of words, and therefore the mystic experience is always ineffable.

Perhaps the best analogy of such an experience that transcends language is the experience of a newborn child who comes into an alien world and is without any understanding from which they might find security. Still, the newborn finds security in the fact that another, of whom they know nothing, is holding them. Their security comes out of the raw experience itself and not out of any understanding of the experience. This is the great unknowing of the mystic experience, an experience that we cannot know but only experience. This analogy is especially appropriate in light of Jesus telling us that we cannot enter the kingdom of heaven unless we become as little children.[3] Indeed, the intention of the "born again" experience is to bring us to a new infancy, where we know nothing of the spiritual world we are entering, and we must become as infants who simply trust the experience of someone holding us.

If God is to make us into the Divine likeness, we must return to the self that God initially created before the world got a hold of us and began shaping us into its likeness by accepting the prejudices that it purports as truth. Return to the pure consciousness of our soul is what Jesus speaks of in John's Gospel where he tells Nicodemus "no one can see the kingdom of God without being

2. Ps 46:10.
3. Matthew 18:3.

born from above."[4] Jesus goes on to say, "What is born of flesh is flesh, and what is born of Spirit is spirit."[5] The flesh is that form of being or identity that we have created in order to survive and thrive in the world, but the kingdom of God of which Jesus speaks requires a different identity in God rather than who we are in the world. Jesus refers to this different identity, or way to be, as being born of the spirit. The spirit is the pure consciousness that God created at our core and that we share with the Divine consciousness that Jesus refers to as the Father. This return to pure consciousness is a return to that innocence where we have nothing figured out, and we have to trust another to whom we seem to be intimately connected. The child's faith is in that other person rather than in themselves and their own understanding. This is the mystic experience and prayer at its deepest level. It is not a matter of our focusing on who we believe God to be, but the deep sense of our connection to the Divine. It is a matter of getting beneath all the layers we imagine we are in order to get to our soul and who we are in God.

The great medieval Christian mystic, Meister Eckhart (1260-1328) claimed that the "eye with which we see God is the same eye with which God sees us." That does not make much sense until we realize that the eye that sees God and the eye through which God sees us is the eye of consciousness itself, which is who we are at our deepest core. It is the pure spiritual seeing of one consciousness connected to another and to nothing else. This is as good a definition of prayer as I can imagine. This experience of our conscious connection to the very consciousness that holds

---

4. John 3:3.
5. John 3:6.

everything together provides a sense of security that is very different from the kind of pseudo security that comes from our claims to knowledge. Of course, there is much more to this idea of prayer to which we now turn our attention.

CHAPTER THREE

Prayer and Identity

PRAYER, IN ITS ULTIMATE FORM, is about identity. It is about getting us to that place at the core of our being where we identify with God rather than with who we are in the world. In its most meaningful form, prayer is not a matter of making petitions to God in order to get our desires fulfilled in order to make us happy. Prayer is that altered state of awareness that takes us into our soul or the pure consciousness that we share with God. In that place, where the things that generally occupy our attention and focus are no longer present, we experience the closeness of a place, where there is nothing between God and us. People have long thought of that thin place, where there is not much between God and us, in terms of geography and have made pilgrimages to various geographical places in order to get closer to God. The mystics, however, have always thought of that thin place in terms of the kind of deep prayer that the mystics practice.

It is the most beautiful and special place that human beings can experience since it is the only place where only God and you can go. It is our uncluttered mind, which is able to experience the Divine presence that is always there but seldom realized. As we have said, the way we get to that place is by sitting in the silence long enough that it silences us. The connection is always there but we seldom experience it because the world around us constantly demands our attention. Of course, the fact that we are constantly aware of the world around us is essential to our physical survival. That was certainly true of our more primitive existence in the wild, but it has only increased with advancing civilization. Human beings today, at least in parts of the world, may not have to be constantly aware of wild animals, scarcity of food, or fear of enemies attacking in the night; yet our fears have not diminished but only increased. We are ever more aware of an enormous pressure to create and maintain an image of ourselves that will be acceptable to the world in which we find ourselves. Our contemporary sociocultural world demands more conformity than our more primitive ancestors could have imagined. In our more primitive state, human beings did not have the pressure and stress of understanding and conforming to the enormously complex set of demands that advanced civilization places upon us. Thus, many people today seek meditation or contemplative prayer as a means of finding momentary peace from the constant barrage of stimuli that demand our attention in order to keep ourselves afloat in an ever-more-demanding world.

The mystic, however, sees their meditation or deep prayer as something much more than finding momentary peace. For the mystic, meditation or deep prayer produces a sense of peace because it puts us in touch with who we really are in God at the core of our being rather than who we are in the world. In the world, we are who others tell us we are. By contrast, the mystic believes that we are who God says we are, no more and no less. Our identity in God is very different from our identity in the world, but in order to realize that identity, we have to experience it firsthand. Prayer is the means of realizing and coming to identify with that deep connection to the Divine. Of course, it is not easy to get to that place. We do not easily dismiss and free ourselves from all those thoughts that constantly possess our conscious attention and keep us from a deeper awareness of the Divine presence at our core.

Many people have no idea that such a place exists. Their normal state of consciousness, constantly flooded with distractions, is their only level of consciousness. When they pray, it is out of that same level of consciousness that they do everything else. The ancient world was wiser. In the culture of Jesus' day, there was a practice originally intended to help people find that deeper level of consciousness, although by the time of Jesus it had degenerated into a mere ritual that Jesus criticizes in the Sermon on the Mount. The practice was fasting, and although we associate it with denying ourselves food, the ultimate intention of fasting was to free ourselves from the distractions that keep us from an awareness of God's presence.

All three of the synoptic Gospels claim that Jesus ministry began with a wilderness experience where Jesus fasted for forty days.[1] Of course, Jesus could have fasted from food without going into the wilderness. Wilderness fasting is not simply a matter of refusing to be distracted by our thoughts of food, but refusing to be distracted by any of the thoughts that so easily occupy our minds because we are constantly looking to other people to tell us who we are rather than identifying with who we are in God.

People who practice fasting from food tell us that after a few days of fasting, the desire for food is no longer the constant

1. Matthew 4:1-11; Mark 1:12-13; Luke 4:1-13.

distraction it usually is. My own limited fasting experiences confirm that report, but wilderness fasting involves much more than
food. My friend, Maggie Ross, whose books have been a great aid
to my own prayer life, spent summers in remote regions of Alaska
fasting from all the distractions the world constantly demands that
we give our attention. After several days in the wilderness, the
diversions that so easily capture and possess our normal level of
awareness lose their grip upon us.

In Jesus' day, however, fasting had become something very
different from Jesus' wilderness experience. It had become a ritual
for some people to show other people how spiritual they were.
Jesus, however, criticizes the fasting of the religious people of his
day, not only because it had become a way to show other people
how spiritual one was, but also because fasting is not about giving
things up for God. Jesus says more than once, "I desire mercy, not
sacrifice."[2] Somehow, we think that God will be pleased if we give
up the things we love, but the only thing God desires from us is
our attention and that is the sole purpose of fasting; that is, to fix
our attention upon God alone.

The experience of God's presence is not simply a matter
or removing distractions, however. It also involves that unique
level of consciousness that we experience when we fall in love.
Anyone who has ever fallen in love recognizes it as somehow
representing a bleep in the normal flow of consciousness. That
is because human beings under normal circumstances cannot fix
their attention on anything for very long, until they fall in love.
The early twentieth century Spanish philosopher, Jose Ortega y

---

2. Matthew 9:13; Matthew 12:7.

Gasset (1883-1955) claimed that love was essentially a matter of attention abnormally fixed. What he claimed was that within the consciousness of the lover there is the constant presence of the beloved.[3] This certainly seems true of people who are romantically "in love," but what he describes seems to encompass many other instances of love as well. The affection children desire from parents involves attention "abnormally fixed." Even friendships, if they are to be meaningful, require that we are capable of fixing our attention upon our friend, and if someone we consider a friend is unwilling to give us their attention, we feel we may have been mistaken in considering them a friend in the first place.

Unfortunately, as much as we desire the attention of spouses, parents, or friends, human beings are not very good at fixing their attention on any one thing for very long. The attention of a normal human being is constantly changing from one object to another.[4] Because of this, we are a constant disappointment to our spouses, children, and friends. A wife often expresses her disappointment in her husband with the words, "You're not here," and although her husband might try to convince her that he was listening and can even repeat what she said, her complaint is still valid. He may have been listening, but he was not attentive. She intuitively knows that love is a matter of attention, and his lack of attention signals a lack of love. Small children seem instinctively to know the same thing and evidence it by clamoring to their mothers, "watch me!"

---

3. Jose Ortega y Gasset. *On Love: Aspects of a Single Theme*. Trans. Toby Talbot (New York: Penguin Books, 1957), 65.

4. Ibid 62-63.

Attention is the great indicator of what we really love. People who love things like golf, money, learning, or sex have little or no trouble fixing their attention on such things for extended durations of time. In fact, most people seem to find it easier to fix their attention upon things rather than other people or God. Because of that, most people are disappointing lovers of their spouses, children, or friends. Indeed, if lovers are ones who fix their attention on their beloved, then the vast majority of human beings are poor lovers, but there is a Divine lover who is always attentively aware of us in a way that no one else can be. Unfortunately, that Divine consciousness that holds everything together and is consciously aware of all that is, generally escapes our notice. Prayer, in its deepest form, is our awareness of God's conscious attention, and our responding with our own conscious awareness of that presence. Richard Rohr calls it "returning the gaze."

In our normal state of consciousness, we are not capable of the kind of attention that prayer involves since our minds experience an endless flow of distractions that demand our attention. We read in Scripture, "Be still and know that I am God," but stilling our mind does not come easily. Thus, prayer is not something we *do,* but a level of awareness that we descend into in order to experience God's presence and respond with our own attentive awareness. Jesus lived his entire life out of this deeper level of consciousness where he was always aware of the Divine presence. Furthermore, this is what he taught his disciples and what is at the base of the Sermon on the Mount and many of his other teachings. Jesus' ministry was about trying to teach others how to live out of that same level of awareness out of which he lived. The essential truth of the gospel is not a set of epistemic beliefs concerning

Jesus' death and resurrection, but the Jesus perspective or level of consciousness out of which he is trying to teach us to live.

When Jesus says that the greatest commandment is, "You should love the Lord your God with all your heart, and with all your soul, and with all your mind,"[5] it is obvious that to do so requires that altered state of consciousness that we only experience when we are *in love*. Of course, we do not maintain that altered state of awareness as Jesus did, or as many of the great mystics did, but the more we visit that place of deep prayer, the closer we get to the Jesus perspective.

Transformation into Jesus' likeness is a matter of taking on the Jesus perspective by learning how to pray from that deepest level of consciousness where there is nothing between God and us. This is the ancient wisdom of the mystics: that Jesus was always speaking out of that place deep within himself where he was constantly aware of the Divine presence. That same place is within all of us. Transformation into his likeness is a matter of learning to identify with, and live out of, that deeper level of consciousness where we are aware of the Divine presence at the core of our being.

That is not the popular view. The popular view is that we do not need transformation into his likeness at all. The popular theory is that we are no longer the object of God's wrath but have become the object of God's love, because we have accepted the fact that Jesus died in payment for our sins. With such a theory, God is the one who changes rather than us. Nothing has changed about us other than the fact that we profess a belief that Jesus died

5. Matthew 22:37.

in payment for our sins, and consequently, God has gone from hating us because of our sins, to loving us because Jesus has paid for our sins. Of course, Jesus does pay for our sin but the payment is not a payment to God but the payment that forgiveness always requires of the innocent to suffer on behalf of the guilty. We will deal with this more extensively in a later chapter. For now, it is enough to see that while Jesus' disciples allowed Jesus' words to transform them and make them into his likeness, many Christians today have little interest in taking on Jesus' likeness. They are content with the belief that they become righteous because of what they believe to be factually true concerning Jesus' death and resurrection. Unfortunately, their idea of truth is not the notion of truth of which Jesus spoke but rather the truth of which Aristotle and the tradition that followed him spoke.

Recall that Aristotle said that truth was merely something to know and has nothing to do with beauty and goodness. Modern science followed in that same direction and taught us to think about truth as what is, regardless of what ought to be because of what is beautiful and good. Jesus' truth is not a set of doctrines to know and believe because they are true, but a truth so divinely beautiful and good that we can fall in love with it. We do not fall in love with something because we believe it to be true. We only fall in love with what we see as beautiful and good, and, we can only see the beauty and goodness of Jesus' words from that deepest level of being who we are in God's presence at the core of our being.

The truth of the gospel is not something to know and believe but a way to *be* because it is divinely beautiful and good. Before the term "Christian" came into use, followers of Jesus identified themselves as people of *The Way*. Jesus said, "I am the way, and the truth, and the life,"[6] and his early followers took that literally. Jesus represented a way to *be* that was divinely beautiful and good as well as true. It was a truth so divinely beautiful and good that those who embraced it treated others as they wished others to treat them.[7] It was a truth so divinely beautiful and good that those who embraced it loved even their enemies and gave to others without expecting anything in return.[8] It was a truth so divinely beautiful that those who fell in love with it were able to rejoice in being poor in spirit, mournful, and meek. It was a truth, which made people hunger and thirst for righteousness, rather than believing that they were righteous because of what they believed.[9] It was a truth so divinely beautiful and good that the early Christians were willing to die to show that it was more beautiful than life itself. It was not a truth that was simply something to know and believe, but rather a truth that was a radically different way to *be*.

Jesus never told us what to believe in terms of theories or doctrines. Instead, he tells us seventeen times throughout the Gospels, "follow me."[10] He is telling us how to *be* as he was. The apostolic followers of Jesus seem to have understood this. They had no theologies or theories of salvation. They simply practiced being like Jesus by making his words their own. Long before the gospel formed into texts, the things that Jesus said passed by word

---

6. John 14:6.

7. Matthew 7:12. This also appears in all of the major world religions.

8. Luke 6:35.

9. Matthew 5:3-6.

10. Matthew 4:19; 8:22; 9:9; 16:24; 19:21; Mark 2:14; 8:34; 10:21; Luke 5:27; 9:23, 59; 18:22; John 1:43; 10:27; 12:26; 13:36; 21:19.

of mouth from one participant in "The Way" to another. Later, when the church was more established, the words of Jesus continued to pass orally through the mass. For the first fifteen hundred years of Christianity, few had the luxury of having the words of Jesus in the form of a text. Today, although the words of Jesus are readily available, many Christians seem more interested in their theologies, theories of salvation, and other portions of scripture rather than the words of Jesus. That should not be surprising since Jesus does not give us what most people want. We want a theology, a theory of salvation, or scriptures that tell us we are righteous before God, while Jesus only tells us that we are in need of repentance for not living the way his words call us to live.

Faith in a doctrine or theory is certainly more popular than the words of Jesus. Our doctrines and theories, however, have changed over time and today there are over forty thousand Christian denominations with a vast variety of theologies, each attempting to explain what the essentials of Jesus' message are. Scientific theories change over time as well, but if there were forty thousand different scientific theories all competing today, we would have trouble believing any of their truth claims. What does not change over time, however, are the perennial words of Jesus, which bring hearers in every generation to repentance and the transformative experience of God's mercy.

Our theologies and theories may comfort us but they do not change us. In fact, they usually do just the opposite and convince us that we are righteous because of what we believe. Jesus' words, however, point us toward repentance and the consequent experience of God's mercy and forgiveness. Unfortunately, we pay little attention to Jesus' words because they make no sense from our normal perspective of who we are in the world. Indeed, they only make sense from the perspective and identity to which Jesus calls us. The perspective and identity to which Jesus' words call us is not compatible with the world and our identity in the world. Thus, the more popular form of Christianity tells us that we can have Jesus and the world and all of its blessing simply by believing that Jesus' death and resurrection have paid for our sins and we are now righteous before God. The only condition for such a belief is that we avoid the words of Jesus that tell us something very different.

A Christianity that is compatible with the world is certainly popular since it seems natural from the perspective of who we are in the world to violently oppose evil, hate our enemies, and expect to get something in return for our giving.[11] As long as we are in the world and identify with who we are in the world, a theology that pays little attention to the words of Jesus and focuses almost exclusively on salvation through his death and resurrection is attractive. Unfortunately, we only come into the fullness of life to which Jesus calls us by falling in love with the words of Jesus, and that, for the most part, is impossible from the perspective of who we are in the world. From our worldly perspective, Jesus' words make no sense, so we ignore them and create theologies and theories of salvation founded merely upon the name of Jesus rather than his teachings. We claim that we love the God of whom Jesus speaks but if that were true, we would love Jesus' challenging words. The truth is that the world hates the words of Jesus and it will hate you if you build your life upon those words. "If the

11. Matthew 5:39-45.

world hates you, be aware that it hated me before it hated you. If you belonged to the world, the world would love you as its own. Because you do not belong to the world, but I have chosen you out of the world—therefore the world hates you."[12]

Without falling in love with the words of Jesus, our response to God can never be more than obedience out of fear. That is not necessarily a bad place to begin but certainly less than the fullness of life to which Jesus calls us. We only begin to realize the fullness of life by giving our attention to his words and making them our own, that can only happen, however, when we see those words from the perspective of who we are in God rather than from the perspective of who we are in the world. Prayer, as Jesus understands it, is that place of being *in* God rather than in the world. It is not about making petitions to change the heart of God, but about changing us in order to see the beauty and goodness of Jesus' words. It is about establishing an identity in God rather than in the world. We only get to that place of prayer by getting out of the world and into God's presence. We see this beautifully illustrated in the gospel when Jesus is in the home of Mary and Martha.

> Now as they went on their way, he entered a certain village, where a woman named Martha welcomed him into her home. She had a sister named Mary, who sat at the Lord's feet and listened to what he was saying. But Martha was distracted by her many tasks; so she came to him and asked, "Lord, do you not care that my sister has left me to do all the work by myself? Tell her then to help me." But the Lord answered her, "Martha, Martha, you are worried and distracted by many

---

12. John 15:18-19.

things; there is need of only one thing. Mary has chosen the better part, which will not be taken from her."[13]

Prayer, in its purest form, is essentially a place where we are aware of the Divine presence and lose ourselves in that presence. In our normal state of consciousness, we are all like Martha, concerned and occupied by a great variety of things. Prayer is that place within us where we are only concerned with one thing, but it is not easy to get to that place of stillness in God's presence. It requires a different level of consciousness where we come to identify with who we are in God rather than who we are in the world.

Mary and Martha are the two long-standing traditions that run throughout the Bible and the history of the Christian church as well. There is the one tradition of trying to do things that will be pleasing to God in order that we might find favor with God and therein see ourselves as righteous, and there is the other tradition of finding our ultimate pleasure in simply enjoying God's presence. The great revelation of the gospel and the fullness of life to which Jesus is calling us is that we have the same ability as Jesus had to realize and live in an awareness of the Divine presence. Martha is aware of Jesus as someone she is trying to please, but she is oblivious of Jesus' presence, because she is too aware of her own presence. We are constantly distracted from an awareness of the Divine presence just as Martha was because we are constantly lost in our own thoughts and concerns rather than lost in the divine presence.

Prayer is a matter of getting lost in God. As we have said, however, this place of prayer is not an easy place to find.

---

13. Luke 10:38-42.

Sometimes it is thrust upon us, and we experience the Divine presence with almost no effort of our own, but usually the distractions of the world keep us from that experience. It is for this reason that prayer requires a practice that does not come easily. If we wish to live out of an awareness of the Divine presence, as Jesus did, we have to learn how to get to that place and spend time there. The more time we spend at that deepest level of consciousness where we are aware of God's presence and nothing else, the more we come to identify with who we are in God and the more we come to see the illusion of the identity we have created for ourselves in the world.

Prayer is that stillness that is capable of experiencing God's presence, but how do we become still? How do we silence all the voices in our head in order to experience the great silence of God's presence? Fortunately, Jesus gives us instructions concerning how to get to this place of prayer. At the beginning of the first of the four Gospels, Jesus' first commandment is, "Repent, for the kingdom of heaven has come near."[14] The Greek word that we translate as repentance is *metanoia*, literally to change your mind. In our Western religious tradition, however, we more often understand repentance as remorse and turning away from sin. It is quite natural that we interpret repentance in that way since human beings initially understand their relationship with God in terms of obedience and disobedience. In the Sermon on the Mount, however, which almost immediately follows from Jesus' call to repent, it seems obvious that Jesus is speaking of repentance as something very different from remorse over failure to obey the traditional

---

14. Matthew 4:17.

Jewish law. The Sermon on the Mount is much more about teaching us to pray, as Jesus understood prayer as a place from which to identify with God rather than the world.

CHAPTER FOUR

The Sermon on the Mount

THE SERMON ON THE MOUNT begins with the Beatitudes, where Jesus tells us that those who are blessed are poor in spirit, mournful, meek, and hungry and thirsty for righteousness. That does not seem to fit with our idea of a blessed life. We spend a lifetime trying to be rich in spirit and avoid mournful situations. We want to overcome our meekness and achieve righteousness, rather than hunger and thirst for it. Jesus certainly seems to be out of touch with the reality of who we are, or at least who we are in that original state in which he finds us. From our perspective in the world, Jesus either is out of touch with reality or sees things from a different perspective than that from which we see things. Furthermore, the things that Jesus says concerning God's prescription for our lives are markedly different from what earlier figures in the Biblical tradition claimed was God's prescription. Prior to Jesus, most of what the Bible tells us about God's prescription for the Jewish people was about their behavior and religious practices, with only occasional hints at something deeper. With the Sermon on the Mount, however, Jesus tells us of God's desire for a relationship based on something very different from right religious practices and the avoidance of sinful behavior. Indeed, Jesus did not relate to God through his behavior or religious practices, but from the very core of his being, and his teachings are always about trying to get his followers to establish their relationship with God on that same basis. Jesus' relationship to God and the world was from a pure heart or pure consciousness, and he tells us that we need to relate to God and the world from that same perspective, rather than the inherited perspective we receive from the world.

In order to understand the Sermon on the Mount, we have to see it from the perspective from which it came. Jesus' perspective is not like ours, which we received as an inheritance from a specific culture and time in human history. Jesus' perspective has come from his prayerful time in his Father's presence, and he is trying to pass that same perspective onto us. At the beginning of the Sermon on the Mount, Jesus tells us, "Blessed are the pure in heart, for they will see God."[1]

> The heart in the ancient sacred traditions has a very specific and perhaps surprising meaning. It is not the seat of our personal affective life ... but an organ for the perception of divine purpose and beauty. It is our antenna, so to speak, given to us to orient us toward the divine radiance and to synchronize our being with its more subtle movements. The heart is not for personal expression but for divine perception. . . .[2]

For Jesus, the heart is that deepest level of pure consciousness where we are aware of nothing but our connection to the Divine presence. Of course, our awareness of God's presence

---

1. Matthew 5:8.

2. Bourgeault, Cynthia. *The Wisdom Way of Knowing: Reclaiming an Ancient Tradition to Awaken the Heart.* (San Francisco: Jossey-Bass. 2003) 33.

goes largely unnoticed because the world and all its distractions constantly occupy our attention. In contrast to us, Jesus was constantly aware of the Divine presence. Consequently, Jesus' words in the Sermon on the Mount and throughout much of the gospel make little sense to us since they represent a level of consciousness to which we are not accustomed. If we are unaware of the level of consciousness out of which Jesus is speaking, we have little choice but to ignore his words and look to other portions of scripture that present us with a level of consciousness to which we are more familiar. Of course, the other option is to understand that Jesus' call to repentance is not one of merely repenting from bad behavior but a call to change our minds and take on the Jesus perspective, which is radically different from whatever socio-cultural perspective we might have inherited. What makes for the enormous spiritual differences between people who consider themselves Christians is how much of the Jesus perspective they have taken on for themselves and how much it has allowed them to make Jesus' words their own.

Taking on the Jesus perspective is largely a matter of becoming aware of the Divine presence as Jesus did. Although God is omnipresent, we are only aware of that presence when we are at the core of our being and beneath all the distractions that usually occupy our conscious attention. Jesus was acutely aware of that divine presence at the core of his being, and he instructs us concerning how we can become aware of it as well. Jesus attempted to teach his disciples how to experience that Divine presence, identify with it, and live out of that experience. That is the main theme that runs throughout the Sermon on the Mount and the Gospels in general.

In the Gospels, as in the rest of scripture, we see people in their relationships with God. Some of those people have a relationship with God based upon an inherited understanding of who God is and who they are in relationship with God. Others have an understanding of God and themselves based upon personal encounters with the Divine. Much of the Sermon on the Mount is about Jesus instructing us concerning how to get to that place where we can experience the Divine presence and enjoy the perspective that such a place provides.

Today, we understand that our experience of the world is perspectival. We can only see what our perspective allows us to see. In order to see more, our perspective has to change. Jesus tries to give us his perspective in order that we might see as he sees. The fact that what we human beings bring to our experience in terms of our perspective largely determines the nature of that experience goes a long way to explain a problem Christians have faced from the beginning. Jesus seems to be introducing a concept of God that appears to be considerably different from what we saw throughout much of the Old Testament. Then Jesus complicates things by insisting that he is speaking about the same God that appears in the Jewish scripture. He further complicates things by both confirming and negating the truth of the Jewish law. He says,

> Do not think that I have come to abolish the law or the prophets; I have come not to abolish but to fulfill. For truly I tell you, until heaven and earth pass away, not one letter, not one stroke of a letter, will pass from the law until all is accomplished. Therefore, whoever breaks one of the least of these commandments, and teaches others to do the same will be called least in the kingdom of heaven; but whoever does

them and teaches them will be called great in the kingdom of heaven. For I tell you, unless your righteousness exceeds that of the scribes and Pharisees, you will never enter the kingdom of heaven.[3]

He goes on to tell us that the law is more than what the Jewish scripture tells us. "You have heard that it was said of those of ancient times, 'You shall not murder'; and 'whoever murders shall be liable to judgment.' But I say to you that if you are angry with a brother or sister, you will be liable to judgment."[4] He then says a very similar thing about adultery. "You have heard that it was said, 'You shall not commit adultery.' But I say to you that everyone who looks at a woman with lust has already committed adultery with her in his heart."[5]

He then says something similar about making oaths.

Again, you have heard that it was said to those of ancient times, "You shall not swear falsely, but carry out the vows you have made to the Lord." But I say to you, Do not swear at all, either by heaven, for it is the throne of God, or by earth, for it is his footstool, or by Jerusalem, for it is the city of the great King. And do not swear by your head, for you cannot make one hair white or black. Let your word be 'Yes, Yes' or 'No, No'; anything more than this comes from the evil one.[6]

Early Christians took this very seriously and died rather than pledging an oath of allegiance to Rome. Today, most Christians

---

3. Matthew 5:17-20.
4. Matthew 5:21-22.
5. Matthew 5:27-28.
6. Matthew 5:33-37.

have no problem pledging an oath of allegiance to the United States of America, which early Christians would have never done because of Jesus' words concerning the swearing of oaths.

Jesus' next amendment to the Jewish law is even more radical.

> You have heard that it was said, "An eye for an eye and a tooth for a tooth." But I say to you, Do not resist an evil doer. But if anyone strikes you on the right cheek, turn the other also; and if anyone wants to sue you and take your coat, give your cloak as well; and if anyone forces you to go one mile, go also a second mile. Give to everyone who begs from you, and do not refuse anyone who wants to borrow from you.[7]

It seems that Jesus is introducing a radically different notion of the law than what Moses had set forth, although Jesus claims that he is not abolishing the law but rather fulfilling it, so what does Jesus mean by claiming that he is the fulfillment of the law? There are several answers to this depending upon what we imagine was God's purpose in creating the law. Our perspective of God's purpose influences how we understand Jesus as the fulfillment of the law. If we believe that the law was given by God to simply make us obedient subjects to God's will, then Jesus is the fulfillment of that obedience even to the point of death. If, however, we think that the ultimate purpose of the law was to create a species of beings that are made after God's likeness in terms of mercy and forgiveness, then Jesus is the fulfillment of the law in that he is the prototype of that new species which God seeks to create. If we understand Jesus being the fulfillment of the law as the prototype for a divine species capable of such intimacy with

---

7. Matthew 5:38-42.

God that they are capable of mercy and forgiveness, then Jesus' words and teachings are instructions concerning how we are to become like him in terms of experiencing the Divine presence and therein becoming merciful and forgiving.

What makes Jesus' revelation so different from everything that came before it is that he understood God's ultimate purpose in giving the law in a way that no one before him ever had. Many never question why God gave us laws to live by in the first place or why God cared about our behavior at all. For many people, it is not a question that needs to be asked. God commanded and it is not our place to question but simply to obey. Some, however, might have understood the law on a deeper level by seeing the law as a blessing from which the Jewish people might establish boundaries and a social identity as a nation. On an even deeper level, we might see the law as part of God's ultimate plan to make us into God's own divine likeness. This seems to be Jesus' understanding of God's ultimate purpose in creating the law.

Prior to the law everyone did what was right in their own minds.[8] Once the law was given, however, it created two very different kinds of people. There were those who abided by the law and were seen by themselves and others as righteous, and those who failed to obey the law and were seen as sinners. If we stop there and that is as far as our perspective evolves, God is all about rewarding obedience and punishing disobedience, but Jesus reveals a deeper perspective concerning God's purpose for the law. From Jesus' perspective, the sinner who disobeys the law and repents is the recipient of mercy and forgiveness, which is intended to make

---

8. Judges 17:6.

them into the likeness of the Divine in terms of mercy and forgiveness. This is the ultimate purpose of the law that Jesus is revealing as he forgives sinners and makes them into his own divine, forgiving likeness for having received much forgiveness.

What we see in the Jesus revelation is that God's ultimate desire is to make us into the Divine likeness in terms of love, mercy, and forgiveness; that only occurs by receiving much forgiveness. Jesus says, "Whoever has been forgiven little loves little,"[9] so, in order to enable us to love much, we need to see how much we have been forgiven. This does not happen by increasing our behavioral sins in order to be forgiven much, but by seeing Jesus as the prototype for who God intends us to be. When we see that Jesus is who God intends us to be, it brings us to an almost constant state of repentance and likewise an almost constant experience of mercy and forgiveness.

The central theme that underlies and runs throughout the Sermon on the Mount and the gospel in general is that God is calling us to something much more than simple obedience and the appearance of righteousness, but rather a deep intimate relationship whereby our awareness of God's mercy and forgiveness makes us into Jesus' likeness. The way that we come to see how much we have been forgiven in order that we might love much is twofold: one, by looking at Jesus as the prototype for the merciful and forgiving creatures that God desires us to become, and two, by Jesus' words which are intended to convince us that our sin is much deeper than we imagine, and likewise our need for mercy and forgiveness is much greater than we imagine.

---

9. Luke 7:47 NIV

Once we see Jesus as the fulfillment of the law and what we are all intended to be, we realize what Jesus means when he tells us that, "Unless your righteousness exceeds that of the scribes and Pharisees, you will never enter the kingdom of heaven."[10] Scholars tell us that the Pharisees of Jesus' day probably kept the Jewish law better than any Jews who had ever lived. What they did not understand, however, was that obedience was not the ultimate purpose of the law. God's desire was not to create a species of obedient creatures but a species of beings made in God's own merciful and forgiving likeness, which Jesus reveals as the fulfillment of the law.

Of course, there is more to being made into Jesus' likeness than merely becoming aware of receiving much mercy and forgiveness for our failure to achieve that likeness. We have to pay attention to Jesus' words but those words make little sense to our normal level of consciousness and our place in the world. Indeed, in order to see how beautiful Jesus' words are they have to be seen from the same level of consciousness from which they came.

Jesus' words came out of his intimate relationship with God, who he refers to as his "Father" and we need to receive those words at that same level of intimacy. At this we balk and are quick to point out that Jesus was God's son and God was his Father but this is not a level of intimacy to which human beings can aspire. Indeed, the reason Jesus was killed by the religious people of his day was that they saw Jesus' claim of God being his own father as blasphemy, and how much more blasphemous would it be for us to make such a claim.

---

10. Matthew 5:20.

Although Jesus refers to God as his Father, with the implication that he is the son of God, he just as often refers to God as *our* Father. In the Sermon on the Mount, he mentions that God is *our* Father sixteen times.[11] Jesus is acutely aware of the fact that he is God's son and he is trying to make us aware of the fact that we are, as well. Our sin is that we are not living out of that identity but out of our identity of who we are in the world. This is the context for nearly all of Jesus' teachings but it is especially obvious in the Sermon on the Mount. Jesus is trying to teach us how to live out of that identity that we have in God rather than the identity we have in the world. The way we come to an awareness of our identity in God is through prayer, and although the Lord's Prayer is at the center of the Sermon on the Mount, the entire three chapters that comprise the Sermon are about prayer or the awareness of the Divine presence that Jesus constantly practiced.

Prayer, in its ultimate form, is a matter of becoming aware of the Divine presence, and Jesus instructs us concerning how to practice that awareness. In doing so he tells us that although God is omnipresent, we are constantly distracted from an awareness of that presence by the things of the world. Since we find our meaning in life by identifying with the world rather than who we are in God, we are filled with thoughts of anger,[12] lust,[13] earthly treasure,[14] worry,[15] and judgments;[16] rather than an awareness of

---

11. Matthew 5:16, 45, 48; 6:1, 4, 6, 6, 8, 9, 14, 15, 18, 18, 26, 32; 7:11.
12. Matthew 5:21-22.
13. Matthew 5:27-28.
14. Matthew 6:19-21.
15. Matthew 6:25-26.
16. Matthew 7:1-3

the Divine presence. Our real sin is that God is not in all of our thoughts, and our identity is in the world rather than in God. Jesus' identity was in God and he lived out of that identity rather than who he was in the world. He is always calls us to that same identity in God.

Our real sin is that our lives are our own creation and we have shaped them around our anger, lust, earthly treasure, worry, and judgments, rather than an awareness of God's presence at the core of our being. Jesus told us that we are not to identify with who we are in the world but who we are as daughters and sons of God. Our failure to do so is our real sin and what keeps us from the fullness of life to which Jesus calls us. He is trying to teach us to live out of the deeper identity of who we are in God.

Righteousness in the form of becoming like our heavenly Father in terms of mercy, forgiveness, and love is not accomplished by obeying behavioral law or believing the right theology, but by seeing how deep our sin really is. Our sin is not in our behavior or even our thoughts; it is in the selves that we have created rather than the self that God has created. In order to discover our true identity in God, we need a repentance that takes us to that deepest level of consciousness where we are aware of the fact that we are God's beloved daughters and sons—no more and no less. This is the underlying theme that runs throughout the Sermon on the Mount and the Gospels in general. It is a call to repentance for adapting to the world and creating a life that will thrive in the world rather than a life created for God's kingdom.

As long as we abide in and identify with the world and the identity we have created to be in the world, we will always operate in its interest rather than the interests of God and his kingdom. At our deepest level of consciousness, which Jesus and the mystics refer to as prayer, self-interest is no longer a concern. From our core consciousness, which connects us to the Divine, we operate out of the interest of God's creation rather than out of the petty interests of who we are in the world. That identity that we have created in order to be in the world is passing away. In fact, we can actually experience it passing away as we age. That is the great blessing of old age; we realize that we are no longer who we wanted everyone to believe we were. Our looks fade, our talents diminish, and our successes are forgotten. We are preparing to enter his Kingdom with only whatever identity we have established in God through our lives.

From the perspective of who we are in the world, it makes no sense to "… love (our) enemies and pray for those who persecute us, so that (we) may be children of (our) Father in heaven."[17] This is not something that we can do with any sincerity when our identity is in the world since, from the perspective of our identity in the world, we see ourselves as very different from our enemies. From the core of our being of who we are in God, however, we can no longer distinguish our enemies from ourselves. Only our tribes and the identities they create for us make us different.

As we have said, Jesus' call to repentance is not about changing our behavior but about changing our minds (*metanoia*) and perceiving the world and ourselves from the perspective of who we are in God rather than who we are in our worldly identity. As long as our identity is in the world rather than God, we will always suffer the sin of hypocrisy. Jesus' notion of hypocrisy, however,

---

17. Matthew 5:44-45.

seems to be different from how most people understand that concept today. We think of hypocrites as people who claim to behave according to certain moral or spiritual standards, while in fact, they do not. Jesus spoke of a different notion of hypocrisy, which tries to convince other people that we have a deep spiritual relationship with God based upon our behavior. Hypocrisy, as Jesus understood it, is the result of one's identity being totally within the world. Thus, hypocrites have no sense of who they are in God at the core of their being. They are no more than the image or persona that they project to other people, God, and themselves. They have a soul but are unaware of it, and therefore without an identity in God at the core of their being, the best they can do is to make a pretense to righteousness through their behavior and the image they project.

Of course, even if we find a deeper identity in God, we often choose to live out of the persona of who we are in the world rather than who we are in God. As in Jesus' day, religious people will always judge us according to their own hypocrisy, and we often conform to it in order to appear righteous in their eyes. Interestingly, Jesus seldom accommodates their hypocrisy and tells us to avoid the appearance of righteousness as well. "Beware of practicing your piety before others in order to be seen by them.... So whenever you give alms, do not sound a trumpet before you, as the hypocrites do in the synagogues and in the streets, so that they may be praised by others."[18] Jesus then says the same thing about prayer.

---

18. Matthew 6:1-2.

When you pray, you are not to be like the hypocrites; for they love to stand and pray in the synagogues and on the street corners so that they may be seen by men. Truly I say to you, they have their reward in full. But you, when you pray, go into your inner room, close your door and pray to your Father who is in secret, and your Father who sees *what is done* in secret will reward you. And when you are praying, do not use meaningless repetition as the Gentiles do, for they suppose that they will be heard for their many words. So do not be like them; for your Father knows what you need before you ask Him.[19]

With prayer, there is a double purpose for going into our inner room. It is not simply to avoid hypocrisy and the appearance of righteousness but more importantly, to avoid all the distractions that constantly bombard us when we are not alone with God at the core of our being. Jesus goes on to tell us that prayer is not essentially about words, but about our inner room. Many people do not know that they have an inner room or secret place where there is communion with God that is beyond words and we need not ask for anything, since the silence of the Divine presence makes any requests we might have seem petty.

Without an awareness of our inner room and the silence we experience there, we are limited to prayers of thanksgiving, intercession, and requests that God change the present circumstances of our lives in the world. Without an understanding of who we are in God, we want God to fix the person we have created for ourselves rather than allowing God to transform us into who God wants us to be. We want answers to our prayers but prayer is not

---

19. Matthew 6:5-8. NASB

about answers but rather about learning a divine way to *be*. In particular, it is about learning how to be aware of the Divine presence and living out of that awareness. Jesus lived his entire life out of a constant awareness of that Divine presence and he is trying to teach us how to attain that same level of awareness that he knew so well. Jesus' conscious attention was rarely distracted from that Divine presence at the core of his being.[20] We, on the other hand, easily succumb to the distractions of the world. Because of that, we have to develop a practice of prayer where we make time each day to seek that presence and that presence alone.

Most people's prayer life, however, is very different from what Jesus is describing in the Sermon on the Mount. Most people pray by talking to God and giving thanks for what they consider blessings and making requests for future blessings. Because this is where we almost all begin, Jesus meets us where we are and gives us an example of how to pray if we insist upon using words. In what we have come to know as "The Lord's Prayer," Jesus outlines the things we should thank God for and the requests we should make concerning future blessings. What he tells us is that: we should declare God's holiness and pray that his kingdom will come upon the earth, that God will provide us our daily bread and forgiveness for our sins, as we forgive others their sins, and that God will deliver us from evil. Strangely, we have chosen to end the Lord's Prayer with verse thirteen and omit the next two verses

---

20. Perhaps the one instance where he was distracted from an awareness of the Divine presence was on the cross where he takes the sin of the world upon himself and cries out, "My God, my God, why have you forsaken me?" Matthew 27:46. When the world overwhelms us with its sin, we can no longer sense the Divine presence, but that presence is always there despite our lack of awareness.

which are perhaps the words of Jesus that are ignored more than anything else he ever said. He says, "For if you forgive others their trespasses, your heavenly Father will also forgive you; but if you do not forgive others, neither will your Father forgive your trespasses."[21] Ponder that for a moment. How does that fit with your theology? Does the Sinners' Prayer or your theory concerning salvation trump Jesus' claim that if you do not forgive others neither will your Father in heaven forgive you?

Throughout these three chapters in Matthew's Gospel that we have dubbed the Sermon on the Mount, Jesus instructs us how to detach from the world, and the identity we have in the world, in order to become aware of the Divine presence at the core of our being. The next thing he mentions is fasting, and he spoke of it in the same way he spoke of almsgiving and prayer. It is not for the sake of making a pretense to righteousness, which he seems to see as the basis of so much of religion. It is not surprising that much of religion is about creating the appearance of righteousness since many people are unaware of being anything more than who they are in the world. They have no idea of who they are in God at the core of their being. Their only identity is the persona they project to the world. Jesus tries to get us to that deeper place in God where we are detached from the world and are consequently aware of God's presence. That is the point of fasting. Prayer is fasting from the distractions that so easily capture and occupy our attention rather than God.

The next thing that Jesus mentions is earthly treasure,[22] which is doubly bad because it occupies our attention as we lust after it

---

21. Matthew 6:14-15.
22. Matthew 6:19-21.

and as we fear losing it. "For where your treasure is, there your heart will be also."[23] Jesus goes on to tell us that, "The eye is the lamp of the body. So, if the eye is healthy, your whole body will be full of light; but if your eye is unhealthy, your whole body will be filled with darkness."[24] What we set our eyes upon are the things to which we give our conscious attention. That is certainly the case with earthly treasure. Jesus, however, tells us that we cannot focus on such things without them becoming the things we serve and give our attention to rather than God. "No one can serve two masters; for a slave will either hate the one and love the other, or be devoted to the one and despise the other. You cannot serve God and wealth."[25]

Jesus then warns us of worry, which few people consider sin. Certainly, worry is something that we all experience. When, however, it takes hold of us, and becomes the distraction that occupies our attention and keeps us from an awareness of the Divine presence, what else is it but sin? The Sermon on the Mount addresses our internal state and never our behavior. This is especially true concerning the next thing that Jesus addresses: judgment.

We spend a great deal of time judging the behavior and motives of others as if we knew the basis for God's judgment. Certainly, we do have our theories concerning God's judgment, but Jesus tells us something shocking. He says that God bases his judgment of us in the way that we judge others. He says, "Do not judge, so that you may not be judged. For with the judgment you

23. Matthew 6:21.
24. Matthew 6:22-23.
25. Matthew 6:24.

make you will be judged."[26] So, the merciful will be judged mercifully, and the judgmental will receive judgment. How cool is that! God allows us to judge ourselves by the way we judge others.

Not everyone thinks this is good news. If the only identity we have is the one we have created for ourselves in order to be in the world rather than to be in God, we want God to judge our righteous behavior in comparison to the evil behavior we see in others, but the Sermon on the Mount is about a deeper level of being. It tries to get us to that place of prayer where we begin to realize our identity in God rather than in the world. Those who have no idea of, or interest in, such a deeper identity in God have little choice but to ignore the Sermon on the Mount. Jesus offers the deeper life of which he speaks to all who desire it, but it does require that we die to who we are in the world. He says, "Knock, and the door will be opened for you."[27] He invites us into that inner life that he shares with the Father, but it is an inner life that who we are in the world cannot experience. We enter into that deeper life in God through what Jesus calls the narrow gate. "Enter through the narrow gate; for the gate is wide and the road is easy that leads to destruction, and there are many who take it. For the gate is narrow and the road is hard that leads to life, and there are few that find it."[28]

Jesus concludes the Sermon on the Mount by warning us of "false prophets, who come to you in sheep's clothing but inwardly are ravenous wolves."[29] Like the rest of the Sermon on the Mount, here we see again the contrast between outer deception and inner

26. Matthew 7:1-2.
27. Matthew 7:7.
28. Matthew 7:13-14.
29. Matthew 7:15.

reality. This contrast between the deception of the outer life of appearance and the inner reality of the spiritual life is the thread that runs throughout the Sermon on the Mount and much of Jesus' teachings throughout the Gospels. The more popular versions of Christianity offer salvation and eternal life for merely believing that Jesus died for our sins. Thus, the Sermon on the Mount is superfluous for those who are merely interested in salvation and a place in heaven. Of course, that is where we nearly all begin, but Jesus' words call us to something more—something deeper that requires a death to who we are in the world in order that a new life in God might come forth.

It is not surprising that we pay such little attention to Jesus' words. We love the person we have created and the idea of that person dying in order for a new life in God to come forth has little appeal, especially for those whose identity in the world appears blessed. In order to maintain that worldly identity, however, we have to ignore the words of Jesus, which constantly point us toward an inner reality, which connects us to the Divine and is so much more than a theology of salvation. He says at the end of the Sermon,

> Not everyone who says to me, "Lord, Lord," will enter the kingdom of heaven, but only the one who does the will of my Father in heaven. On that day many will say to me, "Lord, Lord, did we not prophesy in your name, and cast out demons in your name, and do many deeds of power in your name?" Then I will declare to them, "I never knew you; go away from me, you evildoers."

> Everyone then who hears these words of mine and acts on them will be like a wise man who built his house on rock.

The rain fell, the floods came, and the winds blew and beat on the house, but it did not fall because it had been founded on rock. And everyone who hears these words of mine and does not act upon them will be like a foolish man who built his house on sand.[30]

Jesus' words are the solid rock of which Jesus speaks, yet we pay little attention to his words since they make little sense from the perspective of who we are in the world. We look to other portions of scripture that are compatible to our worldly identity and we ignore those words concerning who Jesus is calling us to be.

The popular forms of Christianity often argue that because Jesus was divine, we cannot aspire to his level of righteousness. There is some truth to that, but Jesus never calls us to righteousness but repentance. That repentance, as we have seen, has the amazing consequence of bringing us to the experience of God's mercy and forgiveness, which, if we experience it enough, makes us into the Divine likeness in terms or mercy and forgiveness. Unlike religious leaders who show us a path to righteousness, Jesus' words always point toward repentance and the transformative experience of mercy and forgiveness. In our normal identity, which Jesus refers to as the flesh, we want to feel good about ourselves. Thus we compare ourselves to other human beings who we see as more sinful than ourselves, rather than comparing ourselves to Jesus in order to become more repentant and consequently more the recipients of mercy and forgiveness.

It is not coincidental that Matthew's Gospel and its Sermon on the Mount are at the beginning of the New Testament because, if

---

30. Matthew 7:21-26.

you do not get the Sermon on the Mount and the kind of repentance to which it calls us, it is hard to understand the gospel message. The central theme of the Sermon is that we are not those individuals that we create out of our anger, lust, reputation, earthly treasure and judgments. We are something deeper than who we pretend to be. We are God's beloved daughters and sons,[31] but we reject that identity and instead set out to create an identity for ourselves. Jesus is interested in getting his followers to understand who they are in God at the core of their being. He is always directing us toward that deeper life in God, rather than who we are in the world. As long as we identify with who we are in the world, it is impossible to make sense of Jesus' words, so we have little choice but to ignore them. As long as our identity is in the world rather than in God, it makes no sense to turn the other cheek and not to respond to violence with violence, to love our enemies, or to give to all who ask expecting nothing in return.[32] Of course, some Christians do abide by Jesus' words but that is usually a good indication that their identity is in God rather than who they are in the world.

We may agree that if we refused to respond in violence and loved even our enemies it would be a heavenly world, but when we view things from the perspective of our identity in this world all that matters is our own private health, wealth, power, or reputation. Who we are in the world cares only for its worldly identity. Even when we act out of kindness, we do so for the sake of increasing our image and status in the world. From the perspective that Jesus calls us to, however, we are absorbed in God and the

---

31. Recall the sixteen times Jesus mentions that in the Sermon on the Mount: Matthew 5:16, 45, 48; 6:1, 4, 6, 6, 8, 9, 14, 15, 18, 18, 26, 32; 7:11.

32. Matthew 5:39-44.

things of his kingdom rather than the things of the world and our identity in it. We are constantly living between these two identities and choosing every moment whether we will be the person we are in God or who we are in the world.

In the Sermon on the Mount, Jesus shows us what our real sin is and that God is not grieved over our behavior, but over the fact that God is not in all of our thoughts and that we choose to live superficial lives, rather than the fullness of life of which Jesus speaks. This should be obvious from the fact that what Jesus mentions in the Sermon are not what Western Christianity generally identifies as sins, but are rather those things that occupy our conscious attention rather than God. Indeed, the teachings of Jesus, and especially the Sermon on the Mount, are not attempting to teach us how to avoid behavioral sins, but rather how to pray and experience communion with God. That is why Jesus tells us at the beginning of the Sermon that, "Unless your righteousness exceeds that of the scribes and Pharisees, you will never enter the kingdom of heaven."[33] The scribes and Pharisees got their behavior right but, as we have seen, Jesus claims that our real sin is not behavioral but the fact that we focus our conscious attention upon the distractions that keep us from an awareness of God's presence at the core of our being.

The other thing that the scribes and Pharisees got wrong, and many Christians today continue to get wrong, is that righteousness is about the avoidance of sin rather than the experience of mercy and forgiveness through repentance. We are only righteous or right with God because of God's mercy and we are only like

---

33. Matthew 5:20.

the Divine in that we are merciful as God is merciful. Jesus shows us in word and deed what real righteousness looks like in order to bring us into a perpetual repentance and consequently the perpetual experience of mercy that transforms us into his merciful likeness. Jesus constantly extends mercy to sinners, not to those who make a pretense to righteousness. This is what Jesus calls hypocrisy, but many who practice hypocrisy cannot see it because we can only see ourselves as the hypocrites we are when we are at the core of our being in prayer.

When we experience God's presence at the core of our being, we are able to see the lie of the self that we project to the world. Jesus' words resonate with our soul but not with who we are in the world. In order to see the beauty of Jesus' words we have to spend time in God's presence at the core of our being, which is the level of consciousness out of which Jesus' words came. At the core of our being, we are God's beloved daughters and sons, no more and no less. From that prayerful level of consciousness, we know nothing about ourselves other than we are somehow in God and God is in us. That is the perspective out of which Jesus spoke and it is the only perspective from which to make sense of his words. This is the ultimate purpose of prayer, to get us to the Jesus perspective in order to see the beauty of his words.

Interestingly, who we are in prayer at the core of our being is also the basis for our rational nature. Human reason, as we generally employ it, is usually not very rational. That is because the essential ingredient of reason is impartiality. Of course, we want to imagine that we are impartial and therefore rational, but the truth is that we constantly reason in the interest of all the prejudices that make up who we are in the world. Pure reason, however, is supposed to be independent of our prejudicial interests. One of the reasons we are attracted to mathematics is because it gives the appearance of operating beneath the level of our prejudices. Such impartiality does seem to be the essential ingredient that underlies rationality, and one of the reasons Plato thought that mathematics and geometry provided the ideal model for what knowledge should look like. Once we move beyond mathematics and geometry, however, it is hard to maintain that same impartiality.

The philosopher, Louis Pojman, in one of his many books, has a great example of reason and its connection to impartiality. He says imagine Notre Dame is playing SMU in football. The two opposing coaches are clearly not rational in the sense that neither is impartial. Both have their own interest at stake and see everything through those interests. The referee, on the other hand, is supposed to be the rational and impartial element in the game. Pojman then interjects the fact that, right before the game, the referee discovers that his wife has their life savings bet on Notre Dame. The question is whether the referee can still be impartial. Pojman's answer is interesting. He says, "He would have to be a very good referee." We are all in the same position as that of the referee. Every decision or judgment we think about making has a direct or indirect effect on us. Thus, when most people reason, they reason from their own self-interest, and merely make a pretense to impartiality by providing evidence to support their position. Nearly everyone does this, but the best among us are able to live out of a deeper level of being detached from the interests of that person they are in the world and make their judgments from the perspective of prayer or who they are in God at the core of their being. We only see the truth to which Jesus is calling us from the perspective of our soul and not from the perspective of who we are in the world. This is the ultimate purpose of prayer: to realize that we have a soul that connects us to God, and the more time we spend in our soul experiencing God's presence the more we come to identify with Jesus' words rather than the world.

Real virtue, like true rationality, always comes from that deeper level of consciousness where we experience our connection to God and all other human beings. Of course, we can act virtuously when we see it is in the interest of who we are in the world. This is what Jesus refers to as hypocrisy. Real virtue is always a core response because of our awareness of who we are in God at the core of our being. We often speak of such people as having character because of their ability to do the right thing regardless of whether it benefits their circumstances or not. The Yiddish word *mensch* describes a person who always does the right thing. In order always to do the right thing, we need a deeper identity than who we are in the world. Jesus is the ultimate *mensch* who is always living out of that deeper identity of who he is in God rather than who he is in the world, and he shows us how to live out of that same place.

Theologians are constantly trying to get the right words to express the *truth* of the gospel, but the gospel is not something to know but a perspective from which we can see the beauty of Jesus' words. The Jesus perspective is the place of prayer and what keeps us from that place are the sins that Jesus mentions throughout the Sermon on the Mount. They are not the cultural sins that the law originally forbade, but the sins that tie us to an identity in the world rather than who we are in God. We build our worldly identity around all the things Jesus mentions in the

Sermon on the Mount: our anger, our lust, our ability to keep our oaths, our worries, and our judgments. By contrast, Jesus continually tells us throughout the Sermon that God is our Father and we are his beloved daughters and sons. This is who we are in God, but to get to that identity and live out of it is not easy. To say that we know and believe that God is our father and we are his beloved daughters and sons is different from *being* that truth. The born again experience is not a magical transformation into a new way of being, but the beginning of a spiritual journey of repentance for constantly falling back into our worldly identity rather than pressing on to the identity Jesus calls us to in God.

The born-again experience is intended to introduce us to a new way of being in God rather than in the world. It involves a new infancy where we need a completely new orientation into a radically different way to be. The words of Jesus provide that orientation but we must become like little children in order to receive that orientation. "Truly I tell you, unless you change and become like children, you will never enter the kingdom of heaven."[34] As long as we remain satisfied with the orientation we received in our first infancy, the words of Jesus will never make sense. Many Christians see no need for such a new orientation. They were born into a Christian culture and therefore they believe they have the proper orientation, but if that were true, they would not avoid the words of Jesus as they do. For many Christians, the words of Jesus are unnecessary and superfluous since Jesus is merely the blood sacrifice that gives us access to heaven. That is an attractive theology since it provides forgiveness without any real change on

---

34. Matthew 18:3.

our part. It allows us to retain our identity in the world and have Jesus too. Jesus as our blood sacrifice might make us grateful but it doesn't change us. In order to come into the fullness of life to which Jesus calls us we need a new identity in God, and that requires a new level of being in God rather than in the world.

CHAPTER FIVE

Being Rather Than Knowing

MANY OF THE GREAT CHRISTIAN SAINTS of the past were agnostics. Of course, their agnosticism was not what we understand by that term today. Today, people claim to be agnostic if they do not outright deny the existence of God but they do not feel they have sufficient evidence for God's existence either. That was not what it meant to be agnostic in the past. In the past, the mystics believed that God existed but they did not believe that we knew as much detail about God as most religious people believed. Certainly, in the past, mystics had to be careful to acknowledge the orthodox beliefs of the day, since the charge of heresy was a serious matter, but what the mystics embraced and put their faith in was the experience of the mystery rather than the conventional theological answers of the day.

The faith of the great Christian mystics was not a faith in what they *knew* about God but a faith in the mystery of both their God experiences and of the gospel. Trusting the mystery is different from trusting what we know and believe. What the mystics put their faith in was a type of prayer that involved direct experience of the Divine. It is a mysterious experience involving a level of consciousness where words do not work. We share our common experiences with words, but the mystic experience is beyond words. Communication with the Divine on the mystic level comes through silence and solitude rather than words. In fact, it is such a different level of awareness that we cannot know it but only experience it. Since the mystic's prayer is that encounter with God in that deep place where only you and God can go, it is unknowable, at least in so far as knowledge is something that we need to have confirmed by others in order to distinguish reality from our own imaginings. For the mystic, the ultimate spiritual reality is beneath that level of knowing. Many mystics report a level of awareness so different from the experiences that we have on our normal level of consciousness that it involves a certain unknowing in order to get to that level of consciousness.

In the *Cloud of Unknowing*, which appeared in the late fourteenth century, we see the anonymous author describe a process of unknowing that allows us to get beyond our inherited socio-cultural understanding of God and the world in order to have raw experiences of the Divine. Faith as a raw, personal experience is unlike knowledge, which is public and shared by many people. Certainly, it is comforting to believe what a great many other people believe, but that does not draw us closer to God. Jesus did not believe what everyone else in his day believed but instead put his faith in the personal experiences he was having with the Father. People who take Jesus seriously have always tried to follow him into the kind of intimate God experiences out of which he speaks.

The mystic's prayer is a very private matter, and because of this, most people look upon the mystic's experiences and the faith they put in them as less substantial than knowledge, since knowledge enjoys a consensus among great numbers of people, but when seen from the broader perspective of history, what we claim to know changes enormously over time. What we claim to know today about the world is very different from what Aristotle or Newton claimed to know. Likewise, our theologies are different today than they were for Thomas Aquinas or Martin Luther. Of course, there are people who see God through the perspectives of such theologians, just as some people still see the world through the perspectives of Aristotle or Newton. The mystic experience, however, is very different. Although uncommon among the population at large, the mystic experience does not change over time the way our ideas concerning what we claim to know changes in order to accommodate the new data that constantly presents itself. Faith, as the mystic understands it, does not produce knowledge, but a perspective or place from which we can see both the divine beauty and goodness of Jesus' words as well as the lie of who we are in the world. It is a faith in that perspective rather than a faith in what we know.

The more popular notion of faith, however, conflates faith with knowledge, in that it presents faith as a set of commonly held beliefs that seem substantial because they are coherent and held by many people, just like knowledge. We establish knowledge on the basis that it is rooted in evidence that is commonly accessible. When we say we believe in certain commonly held religious doctrines and give our reasons for believing such doctrines, we are trying to pass them off as knowledge rather than faith. By contrast, faith, at least as Jesus speaks of it, is private and personal. When Jesus speaks of great faith, it is never about believing what others believe but rather the result of a private experience that reveals a deep and uncommon truth to that individual. There are only two instances in the Gospels where Jesus claims that individuals have great faith. One is a Canaanite woman who knows that God cares for the dogs from the crumbs of the table[1] and the other is a Roman Centurion who has experienced his own power coming from his being under the much greater power of Rome, and consequently he recognizes that Jesus must be under an even greater power than Rome. Both are private experiences and not the kind of beliefs in which many people today put what they call their faith.

A faith in religious beliefs, in addition to appearing more substantial because it more resembles knowledge, since a great number of people endorse the belief, is also more convenient in that it allows us to know God secondhand. Knowledge, unlike faith, is something that we can pass onto others through language without that other person having a personal experience. Someone who has experienced Paris can give us knowledge of it through language, but that is not the same as experiencing it for ourselves. Faith experiences do not travel well from one individual to another since they are experiences we have at our deepest level of consciousness beneath the level of language. We use words to share our common experiences with one another, but the encounters we experience at our deepest level of consciousness are not common, neither are there words in our language to describe the experiences.

Of course, words and the images they evoke also have the function of allowing us to record experiences in memory. Thus, in order to tie their experiences down in memory, the mystics have to use words that attempt to capture and retain the experience in memory, at least for themselves. Although the mystic

---

1. Matthew 15:21-28.

experience is cosmic, the language through which they record the experience is always tribal, and all too easily that recording replaces the original experience. Literalism is the belief that words can perfectly capture our experiences. Aristotle believed something close to that but that is difficult to believe today with what we know about the conventional nature of language. The mystic, apophatic experience seems to be universal although the words used to describe it are always tribal because of the conventional nature of language.

Part of the problem with trying to understand the mystic experience is our belief that it is something that we can know. Many of the great Christian mystics claim that what they experience at the mystical level of prayer is nothing or "no thing". It is empty of content and provides nothing but a divine perspective from which to see. Indeed, it is the only perspective from which we can see the beauty and goodness of Jesus' words. From our perspective in the world, Jesus' words make no sense and we have little choice but to ignore them and find other scriptures that are more compatible with who we are in the world. From the perspective of who we are in God at the core of our being, however, Jesus' words do make sense; of course we can love our enemies and give away all of our possessions in order to follow him. From that place in God, we can turn the other cheek and not respond to violence with violence. When we are in that place of prayer with God at the core of our being, the world no longer has a hold on us. We experience God holding us rather us holding on to what we claim to know. From that place, we can make Jesus' words our own, but we need to spend time in that place in order for Jesus' words to take root within us.

Jesus was aware of this place of prayer and is constantly trying to lead us to that place. We, however, are in the world and its distractions keep us from that sacred place of prayer where only God and you can go. Prayer is the place where we are truly alone with God. It is not a place of knowing but a place of pure seeing—a place of faith. It can initially be a frightening place since it is beneath the level of the kind of knowing in which we usually place our trust. In exchange for giving up that sense of security that comes from trusting what we claim to know, we come to the place from which we can see the beauty of God entering into the world to show us how radically different the Divine is from anything we might have imagined.

From the perspective of who we are in the world, Jesus' teachings are simply ignored; from the perspective of who we are in God at the core of our being, they suddenly become the most beautiful words ever spoken. When you are in prayer where there is only you and God and none of the distraction that usually occupies your conscious attention, you are not concerned about "what you will eat or what you will drink, or about your body, what you will wear."[2] From that place, where you are lost in God, you see the foolishness of all your striving after things that are perishing, and the foolishness of trying to convince others that you are more than you really are. Furthermore, from that ineffable place where you experience the Divine, you see the folly of trying to reduce God to words and human understanding.

Without being familiar with that deeper level of consciousness that is prayer, our ideas of God always remain tribal. We imagine

2. Matthew 6:25.

that Jesus is a member of our tribe and that he sees the world the way we see the world. We imagine that his kingdom resembles Disneyworld but it is restricted and only good people like us are allowed in. If that were true, Jesus' words would make sense to us, but they do not because they speak of a very different world.

The Divine realm of which Jesus speaks is also very different from the religious realm that much of the Bible depicts. Many portions of the Bible portray people responding to God in obedience out of fear, but it also portrays other people moving beyond that religious response of obedience to a response of love; Jesus is that ultimate manifestation of that love response to God. People who respond to God out of obedience, for fear of what God does to the disobedient are in a different place from people who respond to God out of love. These two different relationships with God are dependent upon one's perspective. We may begin with obedience to an all-powerful God but in order to fall in love with God, we have to see the beauty and goodness of God that is manifest in Jesus, but we cannot see that from who we are in the world. We might say that we love Jesus for dying for our sins, but in order to fall in love with someone, we have to see how beautiful and good they are. People who say they love someone because of what the person has done for them are not really talking about love but gratitude. To fall in love with Jesus requires that we see how beautiful and good Jesus is, but Jesus' words appear neither beautiful nor good. From who we are in the world, it makes no sense to love our enemies, to not respond to violence with violence, or to give away all of our possessions in order to follow him. Indeed, we have to perceive Jesus' words from the same level of consciousness from which they came. Jesus identity was not in the *world* but in *God*.

When we get to that place of prayer where our identity is in God rather than in the world, Jesus words make perfect sense.

Of course, this is not where we begin our relationship with God. God initially meets us in our worldly identity. This is where the Bible begins as well. The spiritual journey depicted by the Bible begins with the fear of God: "The fear of the Lord is the beginning of knowledge,"[3] but ends with perfect love casting out all fear. "There is no fear in love, but perfect love casts out fear; for fear has to do with punishment, and whoever fears has not reached perfection in love."[4]

In *The Prince*, Machiavelli claims that when the prince rules through fear, he is in control, but when he rules through the love of the people, they are in control. Thus, those in positions of power tend to prefer and propagate religions based on obedience and fear; consequently, the established church hierarchy often saw the mystic's personal love relationship with God as threats to their power. Perhaps that is a reason for the medieval classic *The Cloud of Unknowing* (circa late fourteenth century) being by an anonymous author. The mystics who did put their names to their works were generally careful not to upset the orthodox beliefs of day for fear of the charge of heresy, which could result in death by burning. When they were not so cautious, they often got in trouble. The German Dominican, Meister Eckhart (1260-1328) had seventeen statements made by him condemned by Pope John XXII. Eckhart appealed the condemnation but died before a verdict was decided. The author of *The Cloud of Unknowing* would have most likely been aware of Meister Eckhart's situation.

---

3. Prov 1:7.
4. 1 John 4:18.

In the *Cloud of Unknowing*, the author presents what we understand much better today than people did in the fourteenth century. That is, that the problem with *knowing* is that it prevents us from *seeing*. Once we believe we know, we can only see what that *knowing* allows us to see. Magicians have been aware of this for centuries but our contemporary behavioral sciences have supported this fact with enormous amounts of evidence. We see through perspectives that limit the scope of what we can see. Since the time of Kant (1724-1804), we have known that we can only see what our mind allows us to see. Once we believe that we know how things work that is what we will see regardless of what is actually before us. The mind is what sees and makes sense of the data that the eyes and other senses admit. Once the mind is full of knowing, only data that conforms to that mind is admissible. The faith of the mystic is a matter of being open to a new orientation and a different level of consciousness beneath all the prejudices that we received through our initial orientation to the world.

The age of the medieval mystics ended with the great Spanish mystics of the sixteenth century, which included Francisco of Osuna (circa 1492/1497—circa 1540), Teresa of Avila (1515-1582), and John of the Cross (1542-1591). The seventeenth and eighteenth centuries brought the Age of Reason and the Enlightenment that was to bolster our confidence in knowledge far beyond what Thomas Aquinas gave to the late medieval world. Throughout the modern period, the mystic influence was limited to the romantic poets and minor Christian mystics like Brother Lawrence (1614-1691) or Madame Guyon (1648-1717). Many people claim that Christian mysticism underwent a rebirth in the twentieth century largely due to the work of Thomas Merton (1915-1968). Merton was certainly instrumental is reviving an interest in mysticism, but perhaps an even more important factor has been the science of the twentieth and twenty-first centuries. Contemporary science has affected our thinking about the world very differently than the medieval science of Aristotle or the modern science of Isaac Newton. Our contemporary science is far more mysterious than what scientists of the past imagined. Both astrophysicists and microphysicists are encountering data that reveal a universe far more mysterious than the data that led Einstein to a mystical perspective a century ago. Unlike the earlier sciences of Aristotle and Newton, which imagined that they were close to figuring out how things ultimately worked, today's science reveals how naïve those attempts at knowing were. Today, physicists use the terms "dark energy" and "dark matter" as placeholders for that which we do not yet have an explanation.

Epistemic truth is always local and dependent upon and relative to the theoretical understanding of the data to which we have access. Newtonian science still works at some level of our experience, but when we consider data that is outside and beyond that theory's ability to make sense, a new conceptual understanding is necessary. Christians should follow the lead of contemporary science and realize that the God that is behind all this is more mysterious than we can imagine, and that the words of Jesus are like the ever-increasing scientific data that confounds whatever understanding we propose as truth. The words of Jesus ultimately reveal how inadequate our normal level of consciousness is in order to understand spiritual truths. That, however, does not mean that the deeper level of being to which Jesus calls us will bring us to such knowledge—quite the opposite. The level of consciousness to which Jesus calls us is beneath the level of knowledge. It is a perspective from which to gaze into the mystery. It is that level of consciousness or place of prayer where we are lost in God.

Jesus constantly calls us to that deepest level of conscious-ness that we share with God and all other human beings. When Jesus tells us that we cannot be his disciples unless, "we hate father and mother, wife and children, brothers and sisters, yes, and even life itself"[5] we balk and think Jesus cannot really mean that, but of course he does. We naturally love our own but that is part of the illusion of being in the world rather than being in the kind of relationship with God to which Jesus calls us. The truth is that our children are not our own but are God's. When we fall for the illusion that they are somehow our creation rather than God's, and we love them more than other children, we are operating out of the illusion of who we believe we are in the world rather than who we are in God. Of course, affection naturally grows for our own children because of the time we spend with them more than other children, but when that affection is based upon the belief that they are our own, we are under the illusion that they are *ours* rather than God's.

If that isn't bad enough, Jesus also tells us that "none of you can become my disciple if you do not give up all your possessions."[6] From the perspective of who we are in the world, such a statement make no sense, and for those who have no other identity besides who they are in the world, it is impossible to hear these words of Jesus. When, however, we spend time in God's presence at the core of our being, our possessions, our enemies, and everything else that

---

5. Luke 14:26.
6. Luke 14:33.

makes up what we think is *our own* fades and we experience our connection to the Divine in the very different light of who we are as God's beloved daughters and sons.[7]

Interestingly, the truth that we experience in deep prayer has almost nothing to do with what we know and believe but everything to do with who we are. We are God's creation, and Jesus is trying to teach us how to live out of a perpetual awareness of our connection to the Divine. Jesus is not trying to give us knowledge. In fact, of the almost two hundred questions asked of Jesus throughout the four Gospels, he answers only a handful.[8] His usual response to a question is to ask a question in return, answer a different question than the one asked, or simply remain silent. We want truth in the form of answers to our big questions, but Jesus refuses to accommodate us. Instead, he reveals in word and deed how to *be*. It is not about knowing but about *being* in God rather than being in the world. This is what the great Christian saints and mystics understood.

To have an identity in God, we have to spend time in God's presence, since it is only from that perspective of who we are in

---

7. Matthew 5:16, 45, 48; 6:1, 4, 6, 6, 8, 9, 14, 15, 18, 18, 26, 32; 7:11;10:20, 29; 18:14; Mark 11:25; Luke 6:36; 11:13; 12:30, 32; John 20:17. Note that in Matthew 6:6 and 18 he mentions it twice.

8. Jesus does answer the following questions when asked: Lord, teach us to pray. (Luke 11:1); What is the greatest commandment? (Matthew 22:37); How many times are we to forgive? (Matt 18:21–22). There may also be an answer to a question with the rich young ruler (Matt 19:16–22). The other two are questionable as to whether they are actually answers. Jesus is asked: "Are you the son of God?" And he answers, "You say that I am" (Luke 22:69–70); Or, "are you the king of the Jews?" To which Jesus again says, "You say so" (Matt 27:11; Mark 15:2).

God at the greatest depth of our being that we can make sense of Jesus' words. Jesus tells us that we are God's beloved daughters and sons, but we have to experience that and not merely acknowledge it as a belief. If we don't actually spend time in mystical union with God, our identity in the world will shape our lives. Indeed, if one is not building one's life around the words of Jesus, the reason is often that they are not spending time in God's presence and therefore are not able to make sense of Jesus' words. Conversion and transformation into the new life to which Jesus calls us is not about acquiring a new set of beliefs but a new way of seeing from that deeper level of consciousness that is prayer. Prayer is that level of consciousness that is similar to the one with which we began our human existence. Just as we came into the world without any understanding, and our only source of security was in the strange experience of someone lovingly holding us, we experience our transformation into the new life to which Jesus calls us not through any understanding of our own but through a similar Divine embrace. Prayer, in its ultimate form, is not a knowing experience but a loving experience, which only requires our attention.

Our attention is what God ultimately desires because God knows that in order for us to come into the fullness of life to which Jesus calls us, we need to experience God's presence and come to identify with who we are in that presence rather than who we are in the world. If we do not get to that place of prayer and the experience of God's presence, we inevitably will identify with who we are in the world. From the perspective of who we are in the world, our theologies and the way we read the Bible usually tell us more about ourselves rather than God. We resonate with the scriptures that speak to where we are in our own spiritual journey and most often avoid the words of Jesus, since they almost never speak to where we are but rather where Jesus is calling us to be. When we find that place of prayer from which Jesus' words make sense, we have found the pearl of great price.

> The kingdom of heaven is like treasure hidden in a field, which someone found and hid; then in his joy he goes and sells all that he has and buys the field.

> Again, the kingdom of heaven is like a merchant in search of fine pearls: on finding one pearl of great value, he went and sold all that he had and bought it.[9]

Jesus tells us, "...the kingdom of God is within you."[10] This is what we discover in the depths of prayer. In the silence and stillness of prayer, we discover our identity in God to which Jesus calls us. John O'Donohue, in his beautiful book, *Anam Cara* says, "To be holy is to be home, to be able to rest in the house of belonging that we call the soul."[11] Learning how to *be* in God at the core of our being is what prayer and faith are all about.

Religions often offer faith as something very different. Religious faith is often a trust and confidence in what we claim to know and believe. That was the nature of the religious people in Jesus' day and things have not changed. Faith in a tradition that we share with many other people appears substantial and affords us a certain sense of security. Religious faith is something to hold

---

9. Matthew 13:44-45.

10. Luke 17:21. ASV

11. O'Donohue, John. *Anam Cara: A Book of Celtic Wisdom.* New York, HarperCollins. 1997. 28.

onto, but faith in the mystery that is God is an experience of some-thing holding onto us. In light of that experience, what we claim to know or believe seems shallow and naïve. The explanations that knowledge offers are attractive to people whose identity is in the world, but they do not get us to the depths of prayer where we can taste the Divine. Without that taste, it is hard to trust that God alone knows, so we seek our security in what we can claim to know and believe.

The Christian religion as a truth to know and believe is very different from the radically different way of being that Jesus taught and modelled. Jesus' teachings were about a way to be in God rather than in the world. That was at the base of the apostolic church but, as Christianity developed into a religion rather than a radically different way to *be*, it took on different dimensions. As it spread from a persecuted group of people who were living in this radically different way, to a movement that even a Roman Emperor would want to be a part of, Christianity began to take on a new form. Although many to this day hail the end of Roman persecution of Christians with Constantine's conversion as a great victory for Christianity, not everyone saw this as a victory. At the same time that Christianity was becoming attractive and accept-able to large numbers of people, others retreated into the Egyptian Desert and lived as hermits to find that deeper life of which Jesus spoke.

Christianity has become something that the world can embrace, but the words of Jesus are always at odds with the world and our identity in the world. From the perspective of our identity in the world we want Jesus to be our savior—but no more. We claim to love the risen Christ who died for our sins but not the

Jesus who calls us to follow him into that deeper life in God. We want salvation but not sanctification.

As long as we identify ourselves with the world, the best we can do in terms of truth is Aristotle's notion of truth as something to know and believe. From our perspective in the world, we cannot know the kind of truth of which Jesus spoke because Jesus' truth is not something to merely know and believe but something to *be*. From who we are in the world, we cannot see Jesus' truth because it requires a deeper perspective than the perspective we have in the world. From our worldly perspective, we see through all the socio-cultural prejudices, conventions, and cultural values that shape our seeing. From who we are in the world, we claim to know and believe many things, but history eventually reveals such knowledge as the prejudices and conventions of a particular time and place. Jesus is usually speaking from the perspective of who we are eternally in God rather than who we are in the world. We can only get to that perspective through faith.

Faith is not like what we claim to know and believe. Faith is a seeing from a deeper level of being. Faith "is not faith that God exists, that life is essentially good, or that this or that is true. All such things are *beliefs*, not faith. Faith is, instead, a way of being, completely open, empty ... of all specifics."[12] Faith is a matter of experiencing God from the greatest depths of our soul. It is from that deepest place within us that Immanuel Kant thought we had to reason from in order to be moral creatures, and the place that John Rawls thought that we had to get to in our imagination in order to see what a just state would look like. Most importantly,

---

12. May, Gerald. *The Dark Night of the Soul*. New York: Harper Collins, 2004. Pp. 191-192.

it is the only place from which to see the beauty and goodness of Jesus' words.

From our identity in the world, we find it impossible to take Jesus' words seriously. We much prefer knowledge to faith and much prefer Aristotle's notion of truth to Jesus' truth. Knowledge and common beliefs are comforting because other people believe what we believe. Faith is frightening because it is something between just you and God, but it does allow you to see things that you cannot see from anywhere else. Indeed, our soul or who we are in God is the only place from which to see what is truly moral, just, and divinely beautiful. Unless we visit this place of prayer on a regular basis, we become who we are in the world, not who Jesus is calling us to be in God.

From our normal level of consciousness in the world, we can understand the God of the Old Testament since that generally depicts who we are in our initial encounters with God where we imagine that God desires obedience, just like human authority. From that normal level of consciousness, however, we cannot imagine a God that desires the kind of loving intimacy that Jesus describes and models. From our normal level of consciousness, the most that we can imagine is a god that is like the gods of this world who reward obedience and punish disobedience, but Jesus tells us that God is "kind to the ungrateful and wicked."[13] We can only understand that from that deeper level of being *in* God to which Jesus calls us. Jesus repeatedly tells us that the God of the universe is "our father" but that makes no sense unless we actually experience the divine embrace, which we can only experience at

---

13. Luke 6:35.

our deepest level of awareness. We all want Jesus to be our savior, especially if it only requires a belief, but we balk at a Jesus who calls us out of the world and into a deeper way of being in God rather than in the world. We all want salvation but sanctification is quite another matter.

CHAPTER SIX

The Parables of Jesus

JUST AS WE DO WITH THE SERMON ON THE MOUNT, we generally ignore the parables of Jesus as well. If we do pay attention to them, we often get the message wrong, since Jesus' teachings are calling us to a radically different way to be. The parables in particular are showing us how different it is to be in God rather than in the world. In order to understand this radically different way to *be*, Jesus tells us that we must begin life anew from a radically different perspective of both God and ourselves. Jesus tries to explain this to Nicodemus in John's Gospel, but it is something that has to be experienced in the midst of the journey; before that, it just sounds crazy.

> Now there was a Pharisee named Nicodemus, a leader of the Jews. He came to Jesus by night and said to him, "Rabbi, we know that you are a teacher who has come from God; for no one can do these signs that you do apart from the presence of God." Jesus answered him, "Very truly, I tell you, no one can see the kingdom of God without being born from above." Nicodemus said to him, "How can anyone be born after having grown old? Can one enter a second time into the mother's womb and be born?" Jesus answered, "Very truly, I tell you, no one can enter the kingdom of God without being

born of water and Spirit. What is born of the flesh is flesh, and what is born of the Spirit is spirit. Do not be astonished that I said to you, 'You must be born from above.' The wind blows where it chooses, and you hear the sound of it, but you do not know where it comes from or where it goes. So it is with everyone who is born of the Spirit." Nicodemus said to him, "How can these things be?" Jesus answered him, "Are you a teacher of Israel, and yet you do not understand these things? Very truly, I tell you, we speak of what we know and testify to what we have seen; yet you do not receive our testimony. If I told you about earthly things and you do not believe, how can you believe if I tell you of heavenly things?[1]

Like Nicodemus, most people have no idea of a second birth and new identity in God. Even people who claim to base their theology on this scripture and the idea of a born-again experience, usually see it as a onetime experience that somehow changes the heart of God from hating us to loving us, rather than the beginning of an entirely different way to be in God rather than in the world. The new life to which Jesus calls us requires a very different orientation than the one we received in our initial orientation to the world. Our orientation to this new life in God comes through the teachings of Jesus, but his words speak of a world so radically different from our own that most choose to settle into religion rather than pursue the spiritual journey to which Jesus calls us. We, like that little four year old who told her mother that she now knew everything she needed to know, believe we now know and have reached the end of the journey. Jesus, however, is constantly telling us that the kingdom of heaven is very different from what we

---

1. John 3:1-12.

imagine and his words attempt to orient us to that very different world and a very different way of being. Indeed, Jesus is trying to give us his own perspective in order that we might see who we are in God rather than who we are in the world. What determines how far we go in the spiritual journey is how much of the Jesus perspective are we willing to take on as our own.

Again, what keeps us from the perspective to which Jesus is calling us is the belief that we already have it. The major purpose of his parables is to convince us that we do not have the Jesus perspective and that the spiritual journey into that perspective is one of almost perpetual repentance. Thus, learning of Jesus is a matter of learning how to take on his perspective in order to see as he sees.

The parables of Jesus, like the Sermon on the Mount, are not telling us that there is something wrong with our behavior but there is something wrong with how we see God, ourselves, and the world. Consider the story Jesus tells in the fifteenth chapter of Luke's Gospel about the Prodigal Son. A man has two sons, the younger of whom asks his father for his inheritance now instead of waiting for the father to die. Many think this is equivalent to wishing his father dead, and perhaps that ultimately is what the younger son is saying. The father, however, agrees to the request and gives half of his estate to the younger son, who squanders his inheritance to the point of being destitute and on the brink of starvation. He decides to return to his father and ask to become a hired servant in his father's house. Upon his return, however, his father reinstates him as his son, which makes his older brother so furious that the older son refuses to go to the party that his father is giving for his younger brother.

Then Jesus said, "There was a man who had two sons. The younger of them said to his father, 'Father, give me the share of the property that will belong to me.' So he divided his property between them. A few days later the younger son gathered all he had and traveled to a distant country, and there he squandered his property in dissolute living. When he had spent everything, a severe famine took place throughout that country, and he began to be in need. So he went and hired himself out to one of the citizens of that country, who sent him to his fields to feed the pigs. He would gladly have filled himself with the pods that the pigs were eating; and no one gave him anything. But when he came to himself he said, 'How many of my father's hired hands have bread enough and to spare, but here I am dying of hunger! I will get up and go to my father, and I will say to him, "Father, I have sinned against heaven and before you; I am no longer worthy to be called your son; treat me like one of your hired hands."'" So he set off and went to his father. But while he was still far off, his father saw him and was filled with compassion; he ran and put his arms around him and kissed him. Then the son said to him, 'Father, I have sinned against heaven and before you; I am no longer worthy to be called your son.' But the father said to his slaves, 'Quickly, bring out a robe—the best one—and put it on him; put a ring on his finger and sandals on his feet. And get the fatted calf and kill it, and let us eat and celebrate; for this son of mine was dead and is alive again; he was lost and is found!' And they began to celebrate.

Now his elder son was in the field; and when he came and approached the house, he heard music and dancing. He called one of the slaves and asked what was going on. He replied,

'Your brother has come, and your father has killed the fatted calf, because he has got him back safe and sound.' Then he became angry and refused to go in. His father came out and began to plead with him. But he answered his father, 'Listen! For all these years I have been working like a slave for you, and I have never disobeyed your command; yet you have never given me even a young goat so that I might celebrate with my friends. But when this son of yours came back, who has devoured your property with prostitutes, you killed the fatted calf for him!' Then the father said to him, 'Son, you are always with me, and all that is mine is yours. [32] But we had to celebrate and rejoice, because this brother of yours was dead and has come to life; he was lost and has been found.'[2]

If we are honest, most of us side with the older brother in this story. His brother has squandered half of his father's estate and now his father has reinstated his brother and has a party for him. The older brother responds in anger because he has been a good faithful son and now the unfaithful prodigal is getting a party in response to his bad behavior. Jesus intends this parable to reveal the all too human understanding through which we read this story. Most of us sympathize with the older brother on the basis that the younger brother did something wrong and is now rewarded. That certainly goes against our idea of fairness. Of course, Jesus' point is that the older brother has the wrong perspective by seeing the situation out of a cultural milieu that believes that we should reward good behavior and punish bad behavior. If our cultural level of consciousness is our only level of consciousness, we attribute that standard to God as well, but Jesus' point is that there is

---

2. Luke 15:11-32.

another perspective that is more divine and allows us to see the beauty of the father's mercy.

The story of the Prodigal reveals two very different perspectives toward God and our relationship with God. From the perspective of the older son, we see someone who wants his father (and, by analogy, God) to be a rewarder of good behavior and a punisher of bad behavior. That is not how the world always works but it should be if a just God were in control. That is how righteous people imagine and desire God to be. Jesus, however, shows us a very different picture of God. Consider how absurd God's mercy is from the perspective of this parable. The one son does it right and that turns out to be bad, and the other son does it wrong and that turns out to be good. Jesus turns the world upside down by telling us that God is very different from what we initially imagine. God's relationship with us is not contingent upon our good behavior but God's forgiveness and mercy and our relationship with other human beings should not be contingent upon their good behavior but upon our forgiveness and mercy.

That is not who people who consider themselves good people want God to be, and it is not who we want to be ourselves. We want our relationships with other human beings to be contingent upon their good behavior and not our mercy and forgiveness. That requires a very different way of seeing the world and ourselves. Indeed, it would require a perspective very different from the perspective we have developed from being in the world, but Jesus is calling us out of the world and into his kingdom. People who see themselves as good people, if they are honest, hate the story of the Prodigal because they identify with the older brother. The main point of the parable, however, is to destroy our identification with the older brother and bring us to Jesus' perspective, which is the father's perspective. Henri Nouwen claimed that if you get the story of the Prodigal right, you get the gospel, and if you do not get the story of the Prodigal right, you do not get the gospel.

Jesus tries to bring us to that deeper level of being where we identify with God and other human beings rather than our own isolated self-interest. The parables of Jesus are good indicators of the level of being and identity out of which we are operating, and where we need repentance in order to get to that divine perspective to which Jesus is calling us. When we are able to repent, not for our behavior, but for living out of that level of being and identity from which we are only concerned with our own self-interest of who we are in the world, we are able to get to that deeper perspective out of which Jesus speaks. If we do not repent and get to that deeper identity in God, we find ourselves ignoring Jesus' words since they make no sense from the perspective of who we are in the world.

The parables of Jesus are stories that usually force us to take sides and identify with different characters in the story. The side we take is usually a good indicator of whether our identity is in the world or on a deeper level of being *in* God. The parables are not about teaching us how to behave but how to see from a divine perspective, which is very different from the perspective we have created for ourselves in the interest of protecting and defending who we are in the world. Like the parable of Prodigal Son, the parable of the Good Samaritan is another example of seeing things from a divine perspective rather than through the worldly perspective of self-interest.

Just then a lawyer stood up to test Jesus. "Teacher," he said, "what must I do to inherit eternal life?" He said to him, "What is written in the law? What do you read there?" He answered, "You shall love the Lord your God will all your heart, and with all your soul, and with all your strength, and with all your mind; and your neighbor as yourself." And he said to him, "You have given the right answer; do this and you will live."

But wanting to justify himself, he asked Jesus, "And who is my neighbor?" Jesus replied, "A man was going down from Jerusalem to Jericho, and fell into the hands of robbers, who stripped him, beat him, and went away, leaving him half dead. Now by chance a priest was going down that road; and when he saw him, he passed by on the other side. So likewise a Levite, when he came to the place and saw him, passed by on the other side. But a Samaritan while traveling came near him; and when he saw him, he was moved by pity. He went to him and bandaged his wounds, having poured oil and wine on them. Then he put him on his own animal, brought him to an inn, and took care of him. The next day, he took out two denarii, gave them to the innkeeper, and said, "Take care of him; and when I come back, I will repay you whatever more you spend." "Which of these three, do you think, was neighbor to the man who fell into the hands of the robbers?" He said, "The one who showed him mercy." Jesus said to him, "Go and do likewise."[3]

We always see ourselves as different from others, because of how we have distinguished ourselves from others in term of beauty, goodness, talent, power, wealth, or fame. When we are

---

3. Luke 10:25-37.

able to identify with who we are in God at the core of our being, we recognize the illusion of all those things that we naively imagined distinguished ourselves from other human beings. From the core of our being, we recognize not only our connection to God but to all other human beings as well.

In the story that Jesus tells of the Good Samaritan, the priest and the Levite read the situation they find themselves in through the righteousness of who they see themselves as in the world. From that perspective, they see themselves as very different from the man on the side of the road who must be a sinner and is now experiencing God's justice. Even Jesus' own disciples asked Jesus whether a certain blind man who had been blind from birth was blind because of his sin or his parent's sin.[4] From their perspective, bad things do not happen to good people but are the result of sin and God's punishment for disobedience. This appears to be the perspective of the priest and Levite and is often our perspective as well. When we see a homeless person, do we wonder what that person must have done to end up in such a place or are we able to see ourselves in such a position because we are aware that at a deeper level of being we are no different from that homeless person? Many religious people to this day see homelessness and poverty as a result and consequence of sin. Of course, that perspective is the consequence of having our identity in the world rather than in God.

By contrast, the Samaritan sees things differently. Interestingly, the Samaritans were a religious group that the Jews hated because of what they felt were the Samaritans wrong

---

4. John 9:2.

religious beliefs. That is one of the problems with religions. Religious people's notion of truth is often Aristotle's notion of something to merely know and believe rather than something to *be*. Religions often tell us that we are different from other human beings because of our beliefs. The Samaritan, however, seems to have a rather different perspective. He does not see the man on the side of the road as different from himself, the way the priest and Levite do. The Samaritan recognizes the man on the side of the road as himself, which is what Jesus means when he says, "you shall love your neighbor as yourself."[5] The priest and the Levite think that the man on the side of the road is not their neighbor. Our neighbors are ones who are like us, and think and believe as we do. That is the tribal view of who we are in the world but Jesus tries to get us beyond that perspective in order to see who we are in God. Most religions are all about trying to convince us that our religion and its epistemic truths, in which we place what we call our faith, make us different from other people.

Remember what the lawyer wanted to know, and what Jesus refuses to answer: how far does this neighbor thing go? Jesus refuses to answer that question and instead is only interested in teaching us how to *be* a neighbor. Unlike the Christian religion, which for two thousand years has told us myriads of different things to believe, Jesus only seems interested in telling us how we should *be*. The Samaritan might not know the right things to believe according the priest and Levite but he knows how to *be*, in a way that they do not know.

What we claim to know about the world, God, and ourselves

---

5. Matthew 22:39; Mark 12:31.

changes enormously over time as new data forces our understanding to adapt, but the way that Jesus taught us to *be* has not changed and when someone takes his words seriously and lives by them, the world beholds the divine. In every generation, when someone decides to get beyond all the individualizing factors that we believe make us different from one another, we come to the place to which Jesus is always calling us.

The priest and the Levite think they have a good reason for passing by on the other side of the road and not assisting the man in distress. They justify their decision because they believe in a god that is very different from the One of whom Jesus speaks. Their god loves the righteous and hates sinners, and it is easy with such a belief to imagine that the man on the side of the road must be a sinner to have suffered such a terrible fate. This is where we almost all begin concerning our idea of god. It is in the interest of almost every culture and society to present us with a god that rewards good moral behavior and punishes bad moral behavior. Such a god certainly contributes to social cohesion and order, but Jesus teaches his followers about a God very different from what we initially imagine.

Jesus turns the world upside down and presents us with a God that is radically different from the gods of this world. This is why when the disciples ask Jesus who is greatest in the kingdom of heaven, Jesus answers by saying, "Truly I tell you, unless you change and become like children, you will never enter the kingdom of heaven."[6] In order to understand the words of Jesus, we have to get back to who we were before the world got hold

---

6. Matthew 18:3.

of us, back to where we experience our connection to the Divine and nothing more. In Luke's Gospel, when the disciples ask Jesus that same question regarding who was greatest among them, Jesus elaborates more fully.

> A dispute also arose among them as to which one of them was to be regarded as the greatest. But he said to them, "The kings of the Gentiles lord it over them; and those in authority over them are called benefactors. But not so with you; rather the greatest among you must become like the youngest, and the leader like one who serves. For who is greater, the one who is at the table or the one who serves? Is it not the one at the table? But I am among you as one who serves."[7]

This is one of the greatest examples of just how counter-cultural Jesus' message is. The greatest is the least and the servant because they have not been deluded by believing what the world told them about themselves. Those we should pity are those who have bought the lie that they are who their wealth, power, fame, talent, beauty, or intelligence tells them they are. That is the lie of the world that Jesus is always trying to expose. The truth is that we are who God says we are, no more and no less. Jesus teaches us how to live out of that identity rather than our identity in the world.

Sadly, much of the Christian religion has based its popularity upon theologies that show it to be compatible with the world, but Jesus' teachings show just the opposite. Jesus shows us how different the kingdom of heaven is from the world. Perhaps the best place to see this is in the twenty-fifth chapter of Matthew's

---

7. Luke 22:24-27.

Gospel. There Jesus offers three parables, each of which gives us two very different ways to interpret the story. The way we interpret the story tells us whether we are reading the parable from the perspective of who we are in the world, or from Jesus' perspective of who we are in God. Consider the first parable of the ten virgins.

> Then the kingdom of heaven will be like this. Ten brides-maids took their lamps and went out to meet the bridegroom. Five of them were foolish, and five were wise. When the foolish took their lamps, they took no oil with them; but the wise took flasks of oil with their lamps. As the bridegroom was delayed, all of them became drowsy and slept. But at midnight there was a shout, "Look! Here is the bridegroom! Come out to meet him." Then all of the bridesmaids got up and trimmed their lamps. The foolish said to the wise, "Give us some of your oil, for our lamps are going out." But the wise replied, "No! There will not be enough for you and for us; you had better go to the dealers and buy some for your-self." And while they went to buy it, the bridegroom came, and those who were ready went with him into the wedding banquet; and the door was shut. Later the other bridesmaids came also, saying, "Lord, Lord, open to us." But he replied, Truly, I tell you, I do not know you." Keep awake therefore, for you know neither the day nor the hour.[8]

When you read the parable ask yourself who are the good virgins that did it right and who are the bad virgins that did it wrong. That may initially appear obvious, maybe too obvious, because we are looking at it from the perspective of who we are

---

8. Matthew 25:1-13.

in the world. From the perspective of who we are in the world, it appears obvious that the good virgins are the wise virgins that made sure they had enough oil for their lamps. They are wise in the ways of the world, but they refuse to share their oil with the foolish virgins and think only of themselves? That seems at odds with what Jesus is constantly preaching. In fact, Jesus always tells us just the opposite. The foolish virgins might be foolish but there is no indication that they are selfish like the wise virgins. How you read the story tells you something about yourself. It seems that what Jesus intends with the parables is to reveal something about ourselves in order to bring us to repentance and the deeper life we have in God and his kingdom rather than the life we have in the world.

The way the parables work is that they bring us into a story and, as we get into it, we identify with certain characters, but what character we identify with tells us a great deal about ourselves. If you identify with the wise virgins and interpret the parable as a message to be wise, do you feel any guilt for not feeling compassion and empathy for those who are not as wise as yourself? If you interpreted the parable as a message to be wise that is probably a good indication that your identity is still in the world. If, on the other hand, you immediately saw the selfishness of the wise virgins, that is probably a good indication that you have spent time at that deeper level of prayer where you recognize your connection to God and other human beings. We all begin interested in nothing more than your own individual salvation, but sanctification into his likeness requires that we see our connection to all of God's children and that requires a deeper level of prayer and identity.

Interestingly, whatever character we identify with should

bring us to repentance rather than a sense of righteousness for being wise, or condemning the wise virgins for not caring about their sisters. We want to be righteous in God's eyes and our own rather than the recipients of mercy and forgiveness, but the life that Jesus calls us to is one of realizing how much mercy and forgiveness we have received in order that we might love much. We see this as well in the next parable Jesus presents in that same twenty-fifth chapter of Matthew's Gospel. In the second parable, Jesus tells a story of a man who went on a journey and summoned his slaves and entrusted his property to them.

> To one he gave five talents, to another two, to another one, to each according to his ability. Then he went away. The one who had received the five talents went off at once and traded with them, and made five more talents. In the same way, the one who had the two talents made two more talents. But the one who had received the one talent went off and dug a hole in the ground and hid his master's money. After a long time the master of those slaves came and settled accounts with them. Then the one who had received the five talents came forward, bringing five more talents, saying, "Master, you handed over to me five talents; see, I have made five more talents." His master said to him, "Well done, good and trustworthy slave; you have been trustworthy in a few things, I will put you in charge of many things; enter into the joy of your master." And the one with the two talents also came forward, saying, "Master, you handed over to me two talents; see, I have made two more talents." His master said to him, "Well done, good and trustworthy slave; you have been trustworthy in a few things, I will put you in charge of many things; enter into the joy of your master." Then the one who

had received the one talent also came forward, saying, "Master, I knew that you were a harsh man, reaping where you did not sow, and gathering where you did not scatter seed; so I was afraid, and I went and hid your talent in the ground. Here you have what is yours." But his master replied, "You wicked and lazy slave! You knew, did you, that I reap where I did not sow, and gather where I did not scatter? Then you ought to have invested my money with the bankers, and on my return I would have received what was my own with interest. So take the talent from him, and give it to the one with the ten talents. For to all those who have, more will be given, and they will have an abundance; but from those who have nothing, even what they have will be taken away. As for this worthless slave, throw him into the outer darkness, where there will be weeping and gnashing of teeth."[9]

This parable seems plain enough when read from the socio-cultural level of who we are in the world. The message is to be productive and God expects a return on his investment. That fits quite nicely with our socio-cultural world, but if we consider a very similar story that Jesus tells in Luke's Gospel, we get a very different reading.

As they were listening to this, he went on to tell a parable, because he was near Jerusalem, and because they supposed that the kingdom of God was to appear immediately. So he said, "A nobleman went to a distant country to get royal power for himself and then return. He summoned ten of his slaves, and gave them ten pounds, and said to them, 'Do business with these until I come back.' But the citizens of his coun-

---

9. Matthew 25:15-30.

try hated him and sent a delegation after him, saying, 'We do not want this man to rule over us.' When he returned, having received royal power, he ordered these slaves, to whom he had given the money, to be summoned so that he might find out what they had gained by trading. The first came forward and said, 'Lord, your pound has made ten more pounds.' He said to him, 'Well done, good slave! Because you have been trustworthy in a very small thing, take charge of ten cities.' Then the second came, saying, 'Lord, your pound has made five pounds.' He said to him, 'And you, rule over five cities.' Then the other came, saying, 'Lord, here is your pound. I wrapped it up in a piece of cloth, for I was afraid of you, because you are a harsh man; you take what you did not deposit, and reap what you did not sow.' He said to him, 'I will judge you by your own words, you wicked slave! You knew, did you, that I was a harsh man, taking what I did not deposit and reaping what I did not sow? Why then did you not put my money into the bank? Then when I returned, I could have collected it with interest.' He said to the bystanders, 'Take the pound from him and give it to the one who has ten pounds.' (And they said to him, 'Lord, he has ten pounds!') 'I tell you, to all those who have, more will be given; but from those who have nothing, even what they have will be taken away. But as for these enemies of mine who did not want me to be king over them— bring them here and slaughter them in my presence.'"[10]

Since the main characters in both stories are noblemen, we associate them with God and the slaves with ourselves. If we read it from that perspective, it seems that God is punishing the slaves

---

10. Luke 19:11-27.

for being lazy and unproductive. That also fits quite nicely with our initial understanding of a wrathful God who must be pleased or we will suffer his wrath. It also fits with a long tradition of imagining God as royalty rather than the lowly peasant that Jesus presents, but doesn't it strike you as strange that the nobleman in both stories say that they reap where they do not sow. Does that really sound like God? In fact, when we look closer we see that in the second story, Jesus is speaking of the historical event of Herod going off to Rome to become king in Judea, but the Jews sent a delegation to Rome to say that they did not want this man to rule over them. The history of the event ends the same way the story ends, with Herod bringing that delegation before him and slaughtering them in his presence.

Scholars have long been aware of the biases involved in trying to read an ancient culture through our own cultural milieu. From the cultural perspective of our contemporary capitalist society, it is easy to imagine the nobleman as God and the good slaves as the productive servants of God, but that is reading the parables through our cultural prejudices or the prejudices of who we are in the world. Of course, Christianity has become the largest religion in the world by showing itself to be compatible with the world and the ways of the world, but that has only been possible by suppressing the words of Jesus which are always at odds the world. We easily believe that the world's ways are God's ways and that we can have the world and God as well. That obviously sells very well in comparison to Jesus' words, which are always at odds with the world and its ways. We want Jesus to confirm what we think is good and negate what we think is bad, but Jesus constantly does just the opposite. Consider the parable Jesus presents in Luke's Gospel.

There was a rich man who was dressed in purple and fine linen and who feasted sumptuously every day. And at his gate lay a poor man named Lazarus, covered with sores, who longed to satisfy his hunger with what fell from the rich man's table; even the dogs would come and lick his sores. The poor man died and was carried away by the angels to be with Abraham. The rich man also died and was buried. In Hades, where he was being tormented, he looked up and saw Abraham far away with Lazarus by his side. He called out "Father Abraham, have mercy on me, and send Lazarus to dip the tip of his finger in water and cool my tongue; for I am in agony in these flames." But Abraham said, "Child, remember that during your lifetime you received your good things, and Lazarus in like manner evil things; but now he is comforted here, and you are in agony. Besides all this, between you and us a great chasm has been fixed, so that those who might want to pass from here to you cannot do so, and no one can cross from there to us." He said, "Then, father, I beg you to send him to my father's house—for I have five brothers— that he may warn them, so that they will not also come into this place of torment." Abraham replied, "They have Moses and the prophets; they should listen to them." He said, "No, father Abraham; but if someone goes to them from the dead, they will repent." He said to him, "If they will not listen to Moses and the prophets, neither will they be convinced even if someone rises from the dead."[11]

This is an amazing parable on so many levels. Christians believe that Jesus rose from the dead; yet they still refuse to listen to his words, just as the parable prophesied. That is because his

---

11. Luke 16:19-31.

words do not give us what we want. We want Jesus to tell us we are good and the values we pursue are good, but Jesus always tells us just the opposite. He always tells us that we are in need of repentance because a life in God is very different from a life in the world. Consequently, we look to other parts of the Bible to confirm our values, instead of allowing the words of Jesus to bring us to repentance for not living out of that deeper reality to which Jesus calls us.

When was the last time your pastor preached on this parable? It is simply too counter-cultural to be preached in America's popular churches or on Christian TV. We want sermons that make us feel righteous and good about ourselves rather than ones that bring us to an almost constant state of repentance for not being who Jesus calls us to be. We want to believe that the rich man's wealth is God's reward for living a righteous life and that Lazarus' poverty is the result of sin. That is how the gods of this world work and we want Jesus to tell us that is how his God works. Of course, Jesus never does. In fact, with this parable it is hard to extract any kind of meaning from our normal level of being in the world. Why is the rich man in torment? It does not seem that he did anything wrong other than the fact that he lived well, and did not seem to notice or care that Lazarus was suffering. Does God really expect us to notice and care about everyone that is suffering? If that is what God demands, then no one is righteous and everyone needs to live in a constant state of repentance. That does not sell well.

We want a Christian religion that allows us to feel good about ourselves, but Jesus calls us to a deeper life in God that brings us into an awareness of the suffering of others. Of course, we can avoid the suffering of others by creating a theology that sees other people's suffering as the result of their sin and God's punishment for that sin. As long as we are in the world that is easy enough to do and we can find many people to support that view with us, but it is hard to maintain that position when we spend time in that place of prayer to which Jesus calls us. The more time we spend in that altered state of consciousness that is prayer the more we feel connected to not only God but all other human beings as well, especially those who are suffering. We can only imagine and share in that suffering from our soul, which is that deep place of prayer that we share with God and all other human beings.

From our normal identity in the world, we feel what others feel who are like us. From that level of identity, we cannot imagine what the homeless feel like because we cannot imagine ourselves ever being in that position. Likewise, from the perspective of our normal identity in the world, we cannot imagine what the prisoner or refugee feels. Compassion is a great Christian virtue but it is very limited by our perspective in the world and our belief that truth is a matter of *what we believe* rather than *who we are.* Real compassion is realized at that level of prayer deep within our soul, from which we are able to see and feel what people feel who are very different from ourselves. This is the Jesus perspective and the place of prayer and identity to which he calls us.

There is something divinely beautiful about entering into the suffering of others, but it requires a deeper level of being in God rather than in the world. Jesus calls us to that deeper level of awareness that reveals who we are in God rather than who we are in the world. That seems to be what is ultimately important to Jesus, as we see in his third parable in that twenty-fifth chapter of Matthew's Gospel. Here Jesus speaks about the sheep and the goats.

> When the son of man comes in his glory, and all the angels with him, then he will sit on the throne of his glory. All the nations will be gathered before him, and he will separate people one from another as a shepherd separates the sheep from the goats, and he will put the sheep on his right hand and the goats on the left. Then the king will say to those at his right hand, "Come, you that are blessed by my father, inherit the kingdom prepared for you from the foundation of the world; for I was hungry and you gave me food, I was thirsty and you gave me something to drink, I was a stranger and you welcomed me, I was naked and you gave me clothing, I was sick and you took care of me, I was in prison and you visited me." Then the righteous will answer him, "Lord, when was it that we saw you hungry and gave you food, or thirsty and gave you something to drink? When was it when we saw you a stranger and welcomed you, or naked and gave you clothing? And when was it that we saw you sick or in prison and visited you?" And the king will answer them, "Truly, I tell you, just as you did it to one of the least of those who are members of my family, you did it to me." Then he will say to those at his left hand, "You that are accursed, depart from me into the eternal fire that has been prepared for the devil and his angels; for I was hungry and you gave me no food, I was thirsty and you gave me nothing to drink, I was a stranger and you did not welcome me, naked and you did not give me clothing, sick and in prison and you did not visit me." Then they also will answer, "Lord, when was it that we saw you hungry or thirsty or a stranger or naked or sick or in prison,

and did not care for you?" Then he will answer them, "Truly I tell you, just as you did not do it to one of the least of these, you did not do it to me."[12]

This, like so much of what Jesus says, does violence to our theologies and the religious beliefs in which we put what we call our faith. Like so much of what Jesus has to say, these words should keep us in an almost constant state of repentance. Unfortunately, however, so much of religion is about creating theologies that will lead us to righteousness rather than repentance. We construct theologies by searching out scriptures that support our arguments to defend our claims to righteousness rather than seeking out the words of Jesus that will bring us to ever-deeper repentance in order to ground our lives in God rather than in the world. In this particular case with the sheep and the goats, people are quick to point out that Jesus is only speaking about our obligations to members of Jesus' family, which we interpret as people who believe what we believe. "And the king will answer them, 'Truly, I tell you, just as you did it to one of the least of those who are members of my family, you did it to me.'"[13] Thus, we can make a pretense to righteousness and claim that we do feed, clothe, and visit those who are sick or in prison who believe the same epistemic truths we believe. Jesus, however, specifically includes the stranger[14] who we do not know, which therefore extends our obligation to everyone. We think we can ignore the suffering of those that are not members of God's family because we can know

---

12. Matthew 25:31-45.
13. Matthew 25:40.
14. Matthew 25:43.

the sheep from the goats—the saved from the unsaved. That is an arrogant confidence in our own understanding, and not faith. God alone can distinguish the sheep from the goats, and we should always see the homeless stranger as Jesus, rather than as a sinner under God's wrath.

Throughout the Gospels, we see that the problem Jesus had with the religious people of his day was that they thought they could know God through their religious tradition rather than through the spiritual journey to which Jesus calls us. Things have not changed and religious people still trust their tradition and ignore Jesus' words, "follow me."[15] Today, religious types reject Jesus' words subtly by looking to other portions of the Bible and arguing that the entire Bible is God's divine revelation, and there is no difference between Jesus' words and the rest of the Bible, but, of course, there is.

Jesus' words are all about a radically different way to be *in God* rather than *in the world*. When Jesus tells us to give up all of our possessions and follow him,[16] we stop listening. We think of our literal possessions as what sustains our life rather than God. Jesus, however, is usually speaking on a spiritual level rather than a material level. In the world, our possessions are the things that give us our identity: our wealth, our academic degrees, the ministries we have developed, and the positive effect we have had on the world all contribute to the illusion of who we want to believe we are. We think that all counts toward who God wants us to be until we read the words of Jesus, and realize that all God really

---

15. Matthew 4:19; 8:22; 9:9; 16:24; 19:21; Mark 2:14; 8:34; 10:21; Luke 5:27; 9:23, 59; 18:22; John 1:43; 10:27; 12:26; 13:36; 21:19.

16. Matthew 19:21; Luke 18:22.

wants is to commune with us at the core of our being in order that we come to identify with who we are in God rather than who we are in the world. When you spend time in that pure consciousness at the core of your being, where there is just you and God, and none of the distractions that make up who you are in the world, you start to take on a new identity in God.

The Gospel is all about losing ourselves in God. This is why Jesus says, "Those who find their life will lose it, and those who lose their life for my sake will find it."[17] This is the true spiritual divide between people. What separates people spiritually is whether they seek life in the world or in God. Certainly, in our early years we are inclined to seek life in the world. What is so exciting about that life is that it is our own creation. Time in prayer and Jesus' words, however, eventually bring us to see that as the illusion it is, and we begin to seek a deeper identity and life in God.

Many Christians have no idea of an identity in God and live exclusively out of who they are in the world. They are similar to the religious people of Jesus' day who wanted a god who rewarded their relative goodness and punished those who they saw as truly despicable because they did not come up to their standard of goodness. This situation has not changed in two thousand years. Most religious people want the same thing today but, as in Jesus' day, the person we are in the world is very different from the person Jesus tells us God is calling us to be. Jesus' call to repentance is not a call to repent of our sins of disobedience to a wrathful God but a radical call to follow Jesus and discover that deeper level of

---

17. Matthew 10:39.

being where we experience God's presence and come to identify with, and live out of, that divine presence at the core of our being.

This underlying theme runs throughout the parables. Like so much of Jesus' teachings, Jesus intends the parables to bring us to repentance for identifying with the world rather than who we are in God. The Prodigal's older brother cares about his share of the estate and not his brother who was dead and now is alive. If we were honest, most of us identify with the injustice done to the older brother, which is a good indication that our identity is still in the world rather than in God, and we are in need of repentance.

Most of us do not see our identification with the older brother as sin and an occasion for repentance. We empathize with the older brother. Not only might he now have to share what remains of his father's estate with his sinful brother, but his status as the good son has been diminished by his father's mercy. This is typical of religious people who seek righteousness rather than repentance. When our identity is in God, our status in the world and in the minds of other people is of little significance. We see a similar situation with the story of the Good Samaritan. The Samaritan recognizes his connection to another human being and he is not concerned with preserving his own righteousness, which the scribe and Pharisee fear losing by coming in contact with a sinner. Jesus calls us to repent, for our lack of love and compassion rather than our concern to adhere to purity codes.

The gospel is a call to an ever-deeper repentance for not loving God and other human beings as we should. Our initial repentance is generally out of self-interest in order to escape God's wrath, but the spiritual journey to which Jesus calls us always leads us to a deeper repentance over not loving God for who God is rather than for what God can do for us. As we have seen, a person who says that they love another person because of their wealth and gifts might say that they love that person but they only love what that person can do for them and not because they see something beautiful and good within that other person. In such a case, the only thing beautiful and good about that other person is what they can do for you. We nearly all begin in just such a place with God. Falling in love with God, however, is very different. It might begin with salvation, but Jesus is always calling us to a transformation into his own likeness and who we are in God rather than who we are in the world. Sanctification is not about becoming sinless but about becoming like Jesus, specifically in terms of mercy and forgiveness, and that requires Jesus' words and our repentant response to them.

Our initial repentance is usually not very meaningful since we do not know what we are repenting for except in order to escape God's wrath. The parables attempt to bring us to repentance for identifying with the world rather than who we are in God. The wise virgins care nothing about their foolish sister but only about themselves. That is who we are in the world. If the wise virgins knew who the bridegroom really was, of course, they would have shared their oil with their sisters because that is what the one who they love would do. Most religious people do not want to know Jesus, but merely a savior and a god that blesses us in this world rather than one who transforms us into beings suitable for his kingdom. We prefer a Jesus who is our savior and nothing more. We want Jesus to be the answer to how to escape God's wrath, but we are not interested in an entirely different way to be, so we ignore his words and construct our theologies around other portions of scripture that allow us to have Jesus and the world as well.

Consider how backwards we get the two parables about Herod because we read them from who we are in the world rather than the perspective that Jesus offers. From our perspective in the world, Herod looks like God, and indeed, the Herods of the world are the gods that rule over us as long as our identity is in the world rather than in the God that Jesus reveals.

In the parable of the rich man and Lazarus, like the parable about the sheep and goats, the sin is that we cannot see beyond our own self-interest because our perspective is from who we are in the world rather than who we are in God at the core of our being. That is the Jesus perspective to which God calls us and from which we can experience the fullness of life that God has for us.

CHAPTER SEVEN

The Truth of Scripture

THE BIBLE IS GOD'S REVELATION of the relationship between the Divine and the human. Perhaps in the past it was possible to believe that it was the revelation of who God objectively is, but that is difficult to believe today. In earlier times we believed, as Aristotle did, that we had something like direct access to the world as it is. Today, since we now know that we filter our experiences through cultural and historical prejudices and conventions that are unique to our particular time and place. Prayer, in its most essential form is a matter of trying to get beneath all those filters, not in order to know anything objectively, but to see God and the world from the same divine perspective from which Jesus saw God and the world.

It is impossible to see and take seriously the words of Jesus without getting beneath those filters. Many people believe that God can bypass those socio-cultural filters and prejudices in order to give us an objective revelation of God himself. There are several problems with that. The first is that any God that we can claim can be contained within human knowledge is an idol and not the God of whom Jesus speaks that always transcends the boundaries of our knowing. Our pretense to knowledge of God is what often keeps us from the words of Jesus, just as the religious people of Jesus' day could not hear Jesus' words because of what they claimed to know about God. Many religious people simply want answers to the question of what must we do to be righteous and escape God's wrath? Such people seldom like the things that Jesus says because his words are always leading us to repentance rather than righteousness and always undermining what we claim to know about God.

The God of which Jesus speaks always exceeds our understanding, and just as we have to change our understanding of the physical universe in order to accommodate the anomalies that constantly appear over our history, Jesus' words are the spiritual anomalies that force us to lose confidence in our own understanding of both God and ourselves. His words draw us deeper into the mystery, which humbles us into something that is useful to God's purpose. What keeps us from the journey as well as God's purposes is the belief that what we know is sufficient. That is a very parochial view but a comforting one that allows us to put our trust in what we know or claim to know. I keep referring to that author who at age four told her mother that she now knew all she needed to know. Most of us did not make such a claim at age four but, at some point in our lives or perhaps at several points in our lives, we come to such a conclusion. Aristotle thought that he had it all figured out and the world agreed with him for hundreds of years, but that all changed in the modern period. Isaac Newton thought he had it all figured out but we continue to discover that there is more to the universe than we previously imagined. With Einstein, we finally had come to a point in human history where it was no longer reasonable to believe that the universe was a mystery that human beings could reduce to our understanding. The universe continues to reveal data that present anomalies to whatever happens to be our current understanding. There is no reason to believe that at some point in the future all the data will be in and there will be no further anomalies to confound whatever our understanding happens to be at that point. Human history has brought us to this place, yet we have trouble embracing this truth. Aldous Huxley beautifully describes the situation.

> Every individual is at once the beneficiary and the victim of the linguistic tradition into which he has been born—the beneficiary inasmuch as language gives access to the accumulated records of other people's experience, the victim in so far as it confirms him in the belief that reduced awareness is the only awareness, and as it bedevils his sense of reality, so that he is all too apt to take his concepts for data, his words for actual things. That which, in the language of religion, is called "this world" is the universe of reduced awareness, expressed, and, as it were, petrified by language.[1]

If we have finally gotten to the place where we realize that the physical universe is beyond our comprehension, how much more must its creator be beyond our ability to know, but like the universe itself, not beyond our ability to experience. Of course, most of us are still under Aristotle's spell and believe that truth is a matter of *knowing* rather than a matter of *being* as Jesus explains and models. Often Christians put their trust in their coherent theologies rather than the words of Jesus, which, if we paid attention to them, always bring us to repentance rather than the sense of

---

1. Huxley, Aldous. *Heaven and Hell.* HarperCollins Publishers, 2004. Pp. 23-24.

righteousness that we get from believing that truth is something that we can know and profess rather than something to *be* by following Jesus.

Our understanding of our experience is always an interpretation through lenses crafted by earlier generations and not simply by God. God may have given us the hardware through which we experience everything, but the software is a human inheritance. Once we understand God's revelation in that context, the seemingly capricious nature of the biblical revelation makes sense. God is the constant but the interpretation depends greatly upon the understanding and level of consciousness through which we receive that revelation. Jesus receives that Divine revelation from that deepest level of consciousness of who he is in God beneath all the socio-cultural influences that seem so present in other characters throughout the biblical revelation. Likewise, Jesus is able to detect those portions of scripture where the biblical characters were able to receive the Divine revelation from that deeper level of consciousness of who they are in God rather than who they are in the world. Jesus knows who he is in God and who we are in God like no other human being before or since. We say that we believe that God is our father but we do not believe it as Jesus did. That is a belief that we continually have to grow into. It is not something to merely know but something to be. Jesus' being was constantly reflecting that perspective of who he is in God rather than who he is in the world, while we seem to have trouble maintaining that perspective, if indeed we ever get to it at all.

The biblical account records people in their relationship with God, but those relationships reflect where those people were at in their spiritual journeys. God meets us where we are in our understanding of who God is and who we are in relationship to God. Jesus is the end of the spiritual journey to which he calls us but we do not get there through belief alone. It requires a death to our identity in the world and transformation into who Jesus tells us we are in God. That end to which Jesus calls us should be the source of a constant repentance within us.

God constantly tries to commune with us but our receptivity is limited by all the filters that come from our being in the world. This is why prayer that gets us beneath those filters is so important. When we get to that place of who we are in God rather than who we are in the world, we are able to make sense of Jesus' words and see how different they are from the rest of scripture. Jesus' words are the result of experiencing God from a different level of being in God rather than in the world. This is why Jesus can say, "You have heard that it was said to those of ancient times, 'You shall not murder'; and 'whoever murders shall be liable to judgment.' But I say to you that if you are angry...."[2] He then goes on to say the same thing about adultery and lust,[3] about divorce,[4] about making oaths,[5] about retribution,[6] and about loving your enemies.[7] In that fifth chapter of Matthew's Gospel, Jesus uses the phrase, "You have heard that it was said," referring to the Law six times. Earlier in that same chapter he said that he did not come to abolish the law but to fulfill it.[8] He is not establishing a new law

---

2. Matthew 5:21-22.
3. Matthew 5:27-28.
4. Matthew 5:31-32.
5. Matthew 5:33-34.
6. Matthew 5:38-42.
7. Matthew 5:43-48.
8. Matthew 5:17.

but a new understanding of that law from the deeper perspective of who we are in God rather than who we are in the world.

Jesus constantly addresses the fact that we think we know God and what God desires, but we can only know that from the perspective of who we are in God, rather than who we are in the world. As we have continually said, the truth of which Jesus speaks is not something to know but a way to *be*, as he was in relationship to God from the core his being. In order to get to that place, we need to live in a constant state of repentance for identifying with, and living out of, the person we are in the world rather than who we are in God. We ignore the Sermon on the Mount and so many of the parables and other teachings of Jesus because they are about a very different way to be. We usually operate out of and identify with the person that we have created in order to deal with the world, while Jesus always tries to get us to that deeper level of being who we are in God.

We need to stop reading Jesus and the rest of the Bible through the perspective of our identity in the world and start reading the Bible through the perspective that Jesus offers. Many people are oblivious of how perspectival our experience is, especially when it comes to the Bible. They imagine that the entire Bible is an objective revelation of who God is rather than God's revelation of our all too human perspective of God. True, something like an objective revelation or prejudice-free experience does occur at that deepest level of consciousness that is prayer. In recording that experience, however, it becomes an interpretation since our words are of human rather than divine origin and reflect the common understanding of a specific socio-cultural tribe or worldview. Readers of scripture, who are unaware of the nature of human language and how our understanding of our experience is shaped by it, fail to see any difference between the experience and the recording of the experience within language. A lack of such understanding is what most people refer to when they say they take the Bible literally; that is, they see no difference between their experience with God or reading the Bible, and their interpretation of those experiences. That is very comforting since it allows us to believe that the prejudices through which we interpret our experiences are God's prejudices as well. It is comforting to believe that God loves and values what we love and value, and hates what we hate. We recoil at the fact that Jesus tells us, "What is prized by human beings is an abomination in the sight of God,"[9] and we choose simply to ignore it and find other portions of scripture that seem to have God confirming our prejudices rather than destroying them.

Likewise, we much prefer our notion of truth to the concept of truth that Jesus sets forth. The cultural concept of truth that we inherit as children is that of facticity. Our earliest education is an orientation to the world, as earlier generations understood it. As children, we have little choice but to accept that understanding of the world as factual. If our understanding of truth never goes beyond that notion of facticity, we read the Bible as a series of facts, but facts have little meaning unless they are in the context of a story. Truth as facts can be convenient, especially if we want those facts to support our own story and the prejudices at the base of our story. In trying to defend our sense of righteousness, we can always find scriptures that support what we are doing. By

---

9. Luke 16:15.

understanding God's truth simply as facts presented throughout the Bible, rather than the meaning of those facts in the context of the larger story that Jesus reveals, we can justify almost anything. Believing that God ordained Joshua's killing of the babies in Jericho allows us to kill the babies in foreign lands, but it does not fit well with Jesus' teachings about loving our enemies. Since we are generally more comfortable with killing other people's babies than loving our enemies, the stories we create to provide a context for the facts we find in the Bible usually suppress the words of Jesus rather than words of Jesus suppressing those parts of scripture that are more compatible with our identity in the world. The goal of much of religion is to create stories or theologies that lead us to righteousness. Jesus' teachings, however, always lead us to repentance rather than righteousness and are seldom about facts. Facts are about what *is* but Jesus' truth is always about what *ought* to be. Jesus tells us stories or parables about who we are so that we will repent or change our minds and become who God is calling us to be. Many Christians do not know what to do with the teachings of Jesus, because they love the world and have profited from it, but Jesus' teachings are in opposition to the world and its ways, and our identity in that world is the very thing of which we need to repent.

Of course, Jesus is not referring to the physical world of nature that God created but the world that human beings have created based upon wealth, power, and prestige. Our sin is ultimately not in our behavior but in our identity in that we claim to be who the world says we are rather than who Jesus says we are. By believing that the entire Bible is God's perfect prescription for our lives, we create theologies that justify who we are in the world. All that is required is that we suppress the words of Jesus and claim that the Bible is showing us how to be righteous rather than repentant. That is easy enough to do simply by focusing on the death and resurrection of Jesus rather than his teachings. Certainly, we want Jesus to be our Savior, but not our Lord. Jesus as Savior simply requires an epistemic belief in his death and resurrection as payment for our sins, while his words require an entirely new identity in God rather than in the world.

Jesus' words are simply too much for us. We do not mind a little repentance over the kind of bad behavior that the rest of the Bible calls us to repent over, but Jesus goes too far. He wants us to repent for being who we are rather than who he calls us to be. As we saw in the last chapter, when Jesus says, "Whoever comes to me and does not hate father and mother, wife and children, brothers and sisters, and even life itself, cannot be my disciple,"[10] he is calling us to repent for something much deeper than our behavior. As we noted, he ends that section in the fourteenth chapter of Luke's Gospel by saying, "So therefore, none of you can become my disciple if you do not give up all your possessions."[11] Our possessions, including our family, are the things that define us in the world and keep us from that deeper identity in God to which Jesus' words call us.

Jesus' words are eternal words that we are able to truly hear only when we are at the core of our being in God's presence. David must have been at the core of his being in order to hear Jesus' words of love toward Saul, even while Saul was attempting to kill David. Several of the prophets must have heard Jesus' words in

---

10. Luke 14:26.
11. Luke 14:33.

order to abandon all of their possessions and live the ascetic life. Of course, most of the Bible is about people encountering God on a more normative level of consciousness that filters everything through what we claim to know. As we have seen, epistemic truth in terms of what know is never eternal nor immutable, but the truth of Jesus' words speak of a way to be that does not change with the vicissitudes of history as do epistemic truths. To find Jesus' words through the Bible is what it means to read the Bible through Jesus rather than reading Jesus in the context of the rest of the Bible. Without that perspective that Jesus offers, we read the Bible from the level of our cultural consciousness or the cultural consciousness of the period depicted in the biblical text rather than the eternal perspective that Jesus offers. We want to believe that we are capable in our natural state to receive God's revelation just as the authors of the Bible were capable of receiving God's perfect and objective revelation. That, however, is not how communication to human beings works.

Communication is always limited by the understanding that receives that communication. Could God have communicated the truths of atomic chemistry to Moses, or Einstein's physics to David? We can only receive what we are capable of receiving. Think of the times your children misunderstood your communication, and sometimes it was impossible for you to correct that misunderstanding because they were not yet at a level of consciousness from which they could comprehend what you were trying to communicate. Think of the times when your children saw you weeping and asked why you were crying, but you could not explain in a way that they could understand at their level of comprehension. Of course, children will often make up an understanding to account for why you were crying but it is only the best they can muster at their level of understanding. A good part of the spiritual journey is about increasing our capacity to receive God's revelation. That increase in understanding only comes by spending time in God's presence and Jesus' words.

The Bible is a progressive revelation that culminates with the Jesus revelation. God is constantly seeking communication with human beings but that communication is constantly limited because of the understanding through which we interpret our God experiences. Much of the Bible is God attempting to communicate with human beings but human beings misinterpreting God's communication. We see this in the Gospels where Jesus, who most Christians believe is God incarnate, speaks directly to his disciples and they misunderstand him.

> When the disciples reached the other side, they had forgotten to bring any bread. Jesus said to them "Watch out, and beware of the yeast of the Pharisees and Sadducees." They said to one another, "It is because we have brought no bread." And becoming aware of it, Jesus said, "You of little faith, why are you talking about having no bread? Do you still not perceive? Do you not remember the five loaves for the five thousand and how many baskets you gathered? Or the seven loaves for the four thousand, and how many baskets you gathered? How could you fail to perceive that I was not speaking about bread? Beware of the yeast of the Pharisees and Sadducees!" Then they understood that he had not told them to beware of the yeast of bread, but of the teaching of the Pharisees and Sadducees.[12]

---

12. Matthew 16:5-12.

If the disciples in their direct experience with God incarnate misunderstood, or interpreted his communication through their limited understanding, how much more the biblical authors and ourselves? This is the reality of the context for human beings' relationship with and comprehension of God. The epistemic truth that we inherit as our orientation to the world is full of strongholds that limit our understanding. Consider how segregationists in the American south practiced a Christianity that could extend kindness and Christian charity to people of color but saw them as natural inferiors because of an ill-conceived inherited notion of race. We are never free from these social and cultural prejudices until we find that place in God where we are nothing but consciousness itself and we have that pure experience of the Divine presence.

Today, we know that all of our human experience that we can reduce to words is an interpretation based on the cultural, historical, and linguistic understanding we bring to our experience. The Bible is the historic record of those human interpretations regarding our human interaction with God. Interestingly, along with those interpretations are the corrections to those interpretations that the prophets provide. Jesus, in addition to being the incarnation of the Divine, is also the last of the great Jewish prophets, and like so many of them, Jesus opposed the religious leaders and priestly caste who tried to please God with behavior and rituals. The prophets understood and communed with God on a deeper level of being that put them at odds with the religious and political leaders of their day who were unaware of that deeper level of being in God. The religious and political leaders did not start killing the prophets with John the Baptist and Jesus. That had been going on for centuries. The fact that David repented and did not kill Nathan when the prophet confronted him was not the general way those confrontations usually played out. The general case was often like that of Herod killing John the Baptist and the religious leaders killing Jesus, all in the interest of preserving a notion of righteousness founded upon all the prejudices that represent the people's inherited epistemic truth.

When religious people, like Nicodemus, realize there is a deeper way of being in communion with God, they cease to be religious people who make a pretense to knowing God. The experience of the Divine from that deepest level of being makes the epistemic truth of what we claim to know seem trite in comparison to that level of being to which Jesus calls us. This is why Jesus was in conflict with the religious leaders of his day, and why throughout the biblical account there is the conflict between the priestly caste and the prophets. They are living out of two very different levels of awareness and two very different ways to be. As long as we operate out of our identity in the world rather than who we are in God, our God experiences will always be an interpretation, since our normal level of consciousness finds its security in knowledge. Knowledge is never a pure experience but an interpretation based on all the prejudices that make up our culture, history, and language communities. The mystic experience of prayer is something quite different. As we have said, it does not give us knowledge but an experience and perspective from which we can see how divinely beautiful Jesus' words are. Our deepest level of consciousness is empty of everything but our awareness of God's presence. It knows nothing but is able to see everything that is divinely beautiful and good. By contrast, our normal level of consciousness is full of knowing and our pretense to truth. Of

course, what we claim to know change over time, but the mystic's prayerful experience and the perspective it provides exists
beneath the level of all of the prejudices that make up what we
claim to know. It is the perennial Jesus perspective that does not
change over time.

We can only see what our perspective allows us to see and
from our normal perspective in the world, we are not able to see
the beauty and goodness of Jesus' words. The words of Jesus are
not good news to who we are in the world. They are always calling
us to that deeper life and identity in God rather than who we are
in the world. Of course, that gospel does not sell well. The more
popular gospel tells us that we do not have to change at all, but we
can change God from hating us to loving us simply by knowing
and professing the right beliefs. The gospel that so many born-
again Protestants and Catholics find appealing is one that claims
that instead of us changing because of Jesus' words, we can cause
God to change simply by believing a certain theory about Jesus'
death and resurrections.

Jesus was aware of his own impending death but he does
not tell us much about its significance. His followers have always
been aware that there was something mysteriously beautiful about
his death on the cross, but because he says little about it, our desire
for knowledge rather than mystery caused theories to develop. Of
course, Jesus does say that he came to "give his life a ransom for
many."[13] He does not explain what that means, however, so theories developed over the history of Christianity. For the first thousand years of Christianity, most of the theories that tried to give

13. Matthew 20:28; also Mark 10:45.

meaning to that statement centered on the idea that Jesus death somehow ransomed human beings from being under the control of the Satan. In the eleventh century, however, Anselm (1033-1109), the archbishop of Canterbury, argued that the ransom had nothing to do with the Devil but was rather a ransom paid to God. Anselm's reasoning was that our sin offended God's honor, which required us to suffer for that offense. According to Anselm, however, Jesus agrees to suffer in our place, and the cross is a picture of Jesus suffering the wrath of God in our place.

God is always beyond our understanding, but since human beings tend to seek security through a pretense to knowledge, we create idols and metaphors to stand in for an ineffable God who always exceeds our understanding. Jesus' metaphor for God is Father, which has the implication of identifying us as daughters and sons of the Divine. Anselm chose instead the metaphor of a medieval king whose power and honor was all-important. We can imagine a medieval king torturing and killing Jesus, but it is difficult to imagine a loving father doing such a thing. Indeed, if we can imagine a father doing such a thing to his son, we may obey such a father out of fear, but we cannot fall in love with such a father. A fearful God may be our first image of God but Jesus is always calling us to an identity in God based upon God's love rather than our obedience.

Furthermore, Anselm's theory is difficult to understand in light of the fact that Christians believe that Jesus is part of a triune Godhead, but Anselm has one element of the Godhead torturing the other over God's honor. Anselm pictures the man, Jesus suffering the wrath of God for all human beings at the hands of a God that cares more about his honor than the suffering of his son.

Another view that seems more compatible with the rest of Jesus' teachings is that Jesus is God and suffers the wrath not of God, but of human beings, and responds by praying for forgiveness for his torturers.[14]

The nature of forgiveness is such that it always requires that the innocent, offended one pay for the offense in order to restore relationship with the one who caused the offense. Forgiveness is so central throughout Jesus' teachings, that it makes sense that his life ended in the greatest possible display of forgiveness. Of course, such a notion of atonement is not very attractive. Jesus tells us to pick up our cross and follow him into that same forgiveness that he reveals from the cross in five places throughout the Gospels.[15] Forgiveness always involves suffering, and as divinely beautiful as it is, it is not something that comes easily to human beings. Indeed, forgiveness requires the death of who we are in the world in order that we might come into the eternal life to which Jesus calls us. As long as our identity is in the world, we find forgiveness difficult if not impossible. If our only sense of who we are is the self that we have created in order to survive and flourish in the world, any offense to that person is intolerable and demands retaliation. Forgiveness is really only possible from the perspective of who we are in God, which sees our identity in the world as the lie that it is. When we are identifying with who we are in God, it is very hard to take offense, and when we are identifying with who we are in the world, we take offense over everything. A good way to test where we are spiritually is how easily and quickly we forgive.

---

14. Luke 23:34.

15. Matthew 10:38, 16:24; Mark 8:34; Luke 9:23, 14:27.

What makes Anselm's theory so attractive, however, is that instead of the cross revealing the kind of forgiveness and deeper life to which Jesus is calling us, it gives us a way to escape God's wrath simply by believing in the factual truth of an eleventh century theory about Jesus suffering God's wrath in our place. It is also appealing because the idea of a wrathful God who is only interested in our obedience is where we almost all begin. When we were children, it was very natural for us to imagine that our parents' wrath was in response to our disobedience and nothing more. We had no way of initially knowing that their displeasure with us was over their concern for us rather than their own wounded egos over our disobedience. Perhaps the worst of human beings punish their children out of the pleasure they get from inflicting pain, but most punish disobedience in the child's interest and not the parent's interests. Of course, it is hard for the child to see that until they get to a later place in their development.

In addition to our parents, nearly all of human authority seems interested in nothing more than obedience and many religious people see God in the same way. God is someone we must obey and when we disobey God, we need to find a solution in order to avoid God's wrath. The primitive solution to avoiding God's wrath in response to our disobedience was to sacrifice human beings as payment for our displeasing an angry God. Many ancient cultures practiced human sacrifices until eventually replaced with animal sacrifices. The ancient Hebrews additionally had the ritual of the "scapegoat" upon whom they would place all of their sins and chase the goat into the desert in order to be free from their sin and no longer under God's wrath. From our human experience, it is very natural to suppose that God desires obedience and punishes disobedience. It is only as we spend time in the Divine presence and Jesus' words that we discover that God desires something much more from human beings than simply obedience.

Equally, from our human experience, we can only imagine loving someone who is beautiful or good, and a God that could love us in the midst of our sin is initially beyond our imagination. It takes a long time for God to convince us that the Divine cannot only love us in the midst of our sin but desires that we become creatures who can love others in the midst of their sin. That is God's ultimate desire and it is what is at the base of the gospel and all of human history. Of course, we do not begin there but God is always willing to meet us in the place where we are at and not the place to which he is calling us. Jesus is willing to be our scapegoat or blood sacrifice if that is what we need in order to approach a God that we imagine is not capable of loving us in the midst of our sin, but God does not need a scapegoat or blood sacrifice in order to love us. That is in our heads and not in God's head. In fact, if God does need a blood sacrifice or scapegoat in order to love us, then when Jesus tells us to love our enemies, he is telling us to do something that even God cannot do. No wonder we love the Old Testament rather than the words of Jesus.

Of course, there is nothing wrong with believing that Jesus is the blood sacrifice that makes us acceptable in God's sight as long as we do not stop there and we realize that is where we might have to begin in our relationship with what we see as an unapproachable God. Jesus, however, is always revealing a God very different from what we initially imagine. It is one thing to love Jesus for what you believe he did for you, but it is another thing to fall in love with Jesus and the God he reveals because you are able to see the things he said and did are divinely beautiful and supremely good.

True, Jesus does take the sin of the world upon himself but that is part of the great mystery of the cross and the mystery of forgiveness, whereby the innocent suffers the offense without retaliation in order to restore relationship with the guilty. The cross is the mystery of forgiveness, and like the universe itself, which we now know exceeds whatever understanding Aristotle, Newton, Einstein, or future generations will concoct, the mystery of the cross far exceeds Anselm's understanding as well. What happened on that cross and the mystery of forgiveness it reveals is beyond the likes of our minds to understand, but not beyond our experience. Like the universe itself, the cross is something we cannot fit within the scope of human understanding but something we stand before in humble awe and allow to transform us. Jesus on the cross is not something to know, but something to behold. It is that pure seeing that we behold from our being in God rather than our being in the world. To believe that we can devise theories to unlock that mystery are always blasphemous and reveal the arrogance of human beings who have not yet been humbled by the silence of God's presence. Theories about what happened on that cross are public and based in a common language. Faith is always private and personal. It is seeing without knowing—a confidence in something beyond ourselves and beyond what we can know. It is a place from where we can see that God provides for the dogs with the crumbs that fall from the table,[16] and that Jesus is under an even greater power than Rome.[17] It is a seeing that is too easily

---

16. Matthew 15:27.
17. Matthew 8:5-13.

forgotten, however, and therefore we must constantly return to that place of prayer beneath all the filters that keep the mystery hidden from us by reducing it to something we can pretend to know. The gospel constantly calls us to a seeing that is beyond knowing. It is a seeing that humbles us and causes us to lose confidence in what we claim to know and who we claim to be. It is also the place from where we can see that we are far from who Jesus is calling us to be.

We may begin the spiritual journey by praying in order to change God but when we begin to see Jesus as the end of the spiritual journey, we pray in order that we might be changed. Who we are in the world wants God to be merciful toward us, but as we spend time in God's presence and Jesus' words, we see that we are the ones that need to become merciful. As long as our identity is in the world rather than in God, we want God to be merciful toward us but not our enemies, and we hate the fact that Jesus tells us that God is "kind to the ungrateful and the wicked."[18] Even more, we hate the fact that Jesus tells us that if we are to be children of God we are to "be merciful, just as [our] father is merciful."[19] As long as we are in the world, rather than in God, we want the secret to eternal life to be a matter of knowing the truth, but truth in terms of knowledge is always beyond us. That is the great wisdom of the mystics as well as the wisdom of twenty-first century science. The universe eventually reveals anomalies that confound our understanding, just as the words of Jesus confound the theologies in which we place our confidence. That is because God's truth is something to be and not something merely to know. Both

18. Luke 6:35.
19. Luke 6:36.

today's science and the mystics throughout the ages agree that the universe and its creator are beyond our provincial notions and theories. From that perspective, the Bible is not the revelation of who God is but who human beings are in their understanding of their encounters with the Divine. If God were knowable, Jesus would have had much more to say about God. Indeed, Jesus has very little to say about God and when he did speak of God, rather than who we should be in relationship to God, it is usually shocking and not what our human experience has led us to imagine about the nature of God.

The way that Jesus tells us to be, however, is not something that we find initially attractive. We much prefer an epistemic truth that is something to know, to analyze, and to believe rather than something to *be*. As something to know, truth is something we can claim to possess, which makes us better than others who do not possess it. If Jesus, however, is the ultimate truth of what it means to be a human being and not merely a ticket to heaven, then Jesus' truth is something that we *pursue* rather than something we *possess*. Truth as something to know may give us a pretense to righteousness, but truth as something to be, as Jesus was, keeps us in a constant state of repentance, and with it the transformative experience of forgiveness and mercy. We need to read the Bible through Jesus' words that he is "the way, and the truth, and the life,"[20] and that "no one comes to the Father except through"[21] the way, and the truth, and the life that Jesus reveals. He is the way that God calls all human beings to be and we can only claim that truth and life for ourselves through participation in it.

20. John 14:6.
21. Ibid.

Primitive religion calls us to repent over our behavior, which we believe offends God because of our disobedience to divine commandments, but Jesus calls us to repent for living out of who we are in the world rather than who we are in God. We immediately balk at that and look to other places in the Bible where the most that people can imagine about God is that he desires good moral behavior and right religious beliefs and practices. From our perspective in the world, we cannot imagine that God desires the kind of intimate relationship with the Divine of which Jesus speaks. We quickly note that Jesus was Divine and therefore the kind of relationship he speaks of with the Divine is beyond our capacity. Indeed, it is beyond our capacity from the perspective of our identity in the world, but from that deepest level of our being that is prayer, we experience who we are in God. From that place, we get a taste of the kind of intimacy with God of which Jesus speaks and we enter into a deeper repentance, not over our behavior, but repentance for not living more fully out of an awareness of our intimacy with the Divine.

Who we are in the world cannot experience that kind of repentance. The best that we can do from our worldly identity is to repent for disobedience concerning behavior or thoughts, but God is not ultimately concerned with making us obedient, just as our parents were not interested in making us obedient although that is what we initially thought. God is interested in the kind of love relationship with us that makes us into the likeness of Jesus. Repentance for failing to achieve that kind of love relationship with God that Jesus models has the amazing consequence of bringing us to the experience of God's mercy and forgiveness, which, if we practice it enough, is the very thing that does make us into God's merciful and forgiving likeness. This is the ultimate purpose of the gospel. God is trying to make us into Jesus' likeness but we only come into that likeness through a perpetual repentance and consequent and ongoing experience of mercy and forgiveness, which is the nature of the spiritual journey to which Jesus calls us.

CHAPTER EIGHT

Two Christian Narratives and the Spiritual Journey

THERE ARE TWO VERY DIFFERENT and distinct Christian narratives at work in America today, but they have very little to do with the traditional distinctions between Catholic and Protestant. The one narrative sees the entire Bible as an objective revelation of God's nature and his prescription for human beings. Thus, they understand Jesus in the context of the rest of the Bible. The other narrative sees Jesus as God's ultimate revelation and reads the rest of the Bible from the perspective of the Gospels. The first narrative considers epistemic truth as something to which we have direct access and the knowing that comes out of that direct access can be trusted. The other considers that we do not have direct access to epistemic truth and that the world and its Creator are far more mysterious than our initial orientation to the world led us to believe.

Of course, in our initial orientation to the world as children, it was essential to our psychological and social well-being that we accepted the interpretation we received from previous generations as true. In our formative years, our socialization and education are all about obedience to parents, social authority, and God. Over time, however, we encounter circumstances that cause us to question the truth of our initial orientation and our conformity to it.

This is true concerning our lives as individuals and the history of our species as well. Within this context, many cling to the truth of their initial orientation and the sense of security that comes from such an identity, while others set out in search of a better way to understand the circumstances of their lives.

Ultimately, this appears to be at the base of the political divide between conservatives and liberals, but equally it appears also to be what is at the base of two very different Christian narratives. The one narrative believes that we have known from the beginning who God is and what he desires from human beings because the Bible provides that truth. According to this narrative, God desires obedience to his law, and disobedience requires punishment. As we have said, this is where we almost all begin since it is compatible with what we experience with parental and social authority. If we never get beyond that notion of authority, the only solution to our disobedience is to suffer for it or have someone else suffer for our disobedience. Scapegoating is a deep psychological phenomenon that often goes on beneath our notice. The ancient Jews made it into a ritual but this strange psychological phenomenon is also prevalent among siblings who are quick to blame their own actions on brothers or sisters in order to exonerate their own guilt. We even see it in many families who unconsciously identify one child as the scapegoat for all the family's woes.

Many primitive people saw natural disasters and defeats with warring, neighboring tribes as the result of God's anger over disobedience. Human sacrifices were attempts at scapegoating in order to pacify God by making payment for a people's disobedience. The biblical account seems to represent a later stage in the development of human consciousness where animal sacrifices and scapegoat rituals replaced human sacrifices in order to appease a God who was offended by disobedience.

This idea of a God whose main interest is obedience has a long history since it is compatible with and advantageous to maintaining hierarchical social authorities that desire its subjects to see obedience as the highest virtue. That is very different from a God who ultimately desires an intimate love relationship with human beings. Of course, an intimate love relationship requires that we give a great deal of time and attention to that relationship and without that time and attention, we generally do not progress beyond a relationship with God based purely on obedience.

This divides churches more than their specific doctrines. Churches whose hierarchies are interested in ministering to people who are looking to have their security needs met are very different from churches interested in promoting spiritual growth. People with great security needs and little time or interest in pursuing spiritual journeys into deeper intimacy with God will seek churches with fixed doctrines and obedience to those doctrines as the ultimate virtue and criterion by which God judges human beings. Church hierarchies that encourage spiritual growth will be less concerned with dogma and epistemic truth and more inclined toward deeper personal experiences and intimacy with God.

Another distinction between these two different types of churches rests upon whether the church is interested in promising its people righteousness or encouraging the repentance that leads to spiritual growth. If righteousness is our ultimate goal, blood sacrifices or scapegoating rituals are a way to achieve a sense of righteousness before God, since someone else has paid for our sin. Jesus as the ultimate blood sacrifice who pays for our sins is very attractive if we desire a sense of righteousness, but such righteousness represents a change within God and not within us. If spiritual growth into a deeper intimacy with God is our aim rather than righteousness, a continual repentance or changing our minds is necessary. Using Jesus as our scapegoat or blood sacrifice is a way to feel innocent and righteous rather than guilty, but guilt is a necessary ingredient in experiencing spiritual growth. It is not guilt over disobedience to God's law but guilt for not being who Jesus calls us to be.

There is nothing wrong with seeing Jesus as our scapegoat or blood sacrifice. As we have said, if that is the only way that we feel we can approach a holy God, Jesus is willing to be our scapegoat or blood sacrifice, but that is not the end of the story; it is only its beginning. It is fine to begin the spiritual journey there, but the words of Jesus always call us beyond that and reveal a God who is able to love us in the midst of our sin and desires to teach us how to be like the Divine in terms of loving others in the midst of their sins. Of course, this narrative is not as appealing to who we are in the world as the story that ends with Jesus being our scapegoat or blood sacrifice. With Jesus as our blood sacrifice as the end of the story rather than the beginning, we no longer see our need for Jesus' words and the repentance to which they constantly call us. It is not surprising that we see these two very different Christian narratives at work in the world, since Jesus prophesied just such a thing.

Do you think that I have come to bring peace to the earth? No, I tell you, but rather division! From now on five in one household will be divided, three against two and two against

three; they will be divided: father against son and son against
father, mother against daughter and daughter against mother,
mother-in-law against her daughter-in-law and daughter-in-
law against mother-in-law.[22]

Jesus' message has certainly produced division: from the
great schism that separated Eastern Christianity from Western
Christianity, to the Protestant Reformation that separated
Catholics and Protestants, to today's divisions into tens of thousands of Christian denominations worldwide. It should not be surprising that we see these countless divisions concerning the truth
of Christianity since epistemic truth is a matter of making sense
of the data before us and over the centuries, as our perspectives
changed, new ways of interpreting the gospel arose. If you think
you believe the gospel that Christians have always believed, you
have a limited view of Christian history. Epistemic truths, whether
concerning science or religion, change over time. What does not
change is the ontological truth concerning our being. The great
division within Christianity has always been between those whose
identity is in the world and those whose identity is in God. That
seems to take us back to the original distinction between believers
and nonbelievers, but it is more complicated today because the
popular strain of Christianity tells us we can have Jesus and our
identity in the world as well.

For the early, persecuted church, such a comingling of identities in both the world and God was not possible, but once a
Roman emperor became a Christian it was easily imaginable that
one could have both. A Christianity that can comingle both Jesus

---

22. Luke 12:51-53.

as savior and the world and its bounty is certainly attractive. After Constantine, one could reap the benefits of being both a Roman and a Christian. Such a combination was enormously attractive and eventually made Christianity the most popular religion in the world. Today those forms of Christianity that sell best are ones that convince us we can have Jesus and the world, but today it is not a Roman emperor that makes this possible but a certain theology known as the Protestant Work Ethic.

German sociologist Max Weber (1864-1920) argued that Karl Marx (1818-1883) was wrong about his theory of how modern capitalism emerged. Weber argued that capitalism had its origin, or at least found a spiritual basis in the Protestant Work Ethics of reformers like John Knox (1505-1572) and John Calvin (1509-1564). Such men based their Christian ethic on two principles: first, that Christians should be industrious in order to avoid idleness, which led to the occasion of sin; and second, that Christians should avoid worldly pleasures, which were also sinful. Knox also added the idea of thrift as an additional virtue.

Weber argued that these Protestant virtues, although not the cause of capitalism, were what gave the capitalist a spiritual legitimacy. Indeed, if one followed this Protestant ethic, and worked hard, did not spend their money on worldly pleasure, and were thrifty, capital or surplus wealth would be the result. Thus, believers in the Protestant work ethic could see wealth as a sign of godliness. In the twentieth century, radio and television prosperity preachers built on this association between wealth and godliness and argued that God wanted all of his children to be wealthy and only a believer's lack of faith kept them from that wealth.

One problem with such a theory is that if God blesses us

with wealth because we are industrious and frugal, what does that say about the poor? If wealth is the result of Christian virtue, then the inference is that poverty is the result of sin, namely not being industrious and spending money frivolously upon worldly pleasures. I remember hearing a famous Evangelical preacher say, "The worst message the poor of this country ever got was that poverty was not their fault." He then went on to say, "Poverty is the fault of the poor." Consequently, religion should encourage the poor to be industrious and frugal rather than to indulge their sin with charity. The problem with such a view, however, is that it is in complete opposition to Jesus' teachings. The Prosperity Gospel's solution to this is simply to ignore the words of Jesus. They love the Bible but are careful to avoid the words of Jesus. The Protestant work ethic and the Prosperity Gospel may see wealth as the result of Christian virtue and faith but it is hard to square those theologies with the actual things Jesus says. Jesus has some very hard things to say about wealth.

> Do not store up for yourselves treasures on earth, where moth and rust consume and where thieves break in and steal; but store up for yourselves treasures in heaven, where neither moth nor rust consumes and where thieves do not break in and steal. For where your treasure is, there your heart will be also.[23]

Of course, many Christians will argue that they are storing up treasure in heaven and that God is blessing them with wealth here as well. That, however, is hard to defend in light of Jesus' statement in Luke's Gospel: "Woe to you who are rich, for you

---

23. Matthew 6:19-21.

have received your consolation."[24] Furthermore, this is not an isolated passage but one that seems to represent Jesus' very consistent position on wealth and poverty.

In the parable of the Sower and the Seed, which we find in all three of the Synoptic Gospels, Jesus tells us, "As for what was sown among thorns, this is the one who hears the word, but the cares of the world and the lure of wealth choke the word, and it yields nothing."[25] Additionally, in Luke's Gospel, Jesus presents us with a parable about a man who sought wealth rather than God.

> The land of a rich man produced abundantly. And he thought to himself, 'What should I do, for I have no place to store my crops?' Then he said, 'I will do this: I will pull down my barns and build larger ones, and there I will store all my grain and my goods. And I will say to my soul, 'Soul, you have ample goods laid up for many years; relax, eat, drink, be merry.' But God said to him, 'You fool! This very night your life is being demanded of you. And the things you have prepared, whose will they be?' So it is with those who store up treasures for themselves but are not rich toward God.[26]

There is nothing objectively evil about wealth. Jesus concern and warnings about it seem to center on the effect it has upon human beings. Recall that money, in addition to being a means of exchange and a store of value (capital), is also a measure of value. In today's world, we measure nearly everything's value in dollars, including the value of human beings. In most people's thinking,

---

24. Luke 6:24.

25. Matthew 13:22; also see Mark 4:19; Luke 8:14.

26. Luke 12:16-21.

our value and identity in the world increases with our wealth. Wealth, along with power and fame are the virtues of a worldly identity. Jesus, however, is always preaching against the deceptive identity such things produce. Jesus is always calling us to a new identity in God rather than who we are in the world. The rich, powerful, and famous may profess a love for Jesus because of the salvation he provides, but it is difficult for them to achieve the identity to which Jesus calls us, since he tells us that it is impossible to have an identity both in the world and in God. "No one can serve two masters; for a slave will either hate the one and love the other, or be devoted to the one and despise the other. You cannot serve God and wealth."[27] "If you wish to be perfect, go, sell your possessions, and give your money to the poor."[28]

It is all a matter of how far you want to go with this Jesus thing. The popular gospel sells salvation at a cost that allows us to have Jesus and the world as well, but Jesus is always calling us to an identity in God rather than in the world. That requires a spirit of poverty rather than the illusions of wealth, power, and fame. It is for this reason that Jesus says the poor are blessed. "Blessed are you who are poor, for yours is the kingdom of God."[29] He tells us, "The Spirit of the Lord is upon me, because he has anointed me to bring good news to the poor."[30] The message he has for the rich is harsh: "It is easier for a camel to go through the eye of a needle than for someone who is rich to enter the kingdom of God."[31]

Of course, there are examples of rich, powerful, and famous

27. Matthew 6:24; also see Luke 16:13.
28. Matthew 19:21.
29. Luke 6:20.
30. Luke 4:18.
31. Matthew 19:24; also see Mark 10:23-25; Luke 18:24.

people whose identity was in God rather than in the world, just as there are numerous examples of ungodly poor people. The point, however, is that our wealth, power, and prestige adds greatly to the distractions that keep us from an awareness of God's presence at the core of our being, while poverty, powerlessness, and an identity in God alone can reduce those distractions. Jesus tells us that you must "be on your guard against all kinds of greed; for one's life does not consist in the abundance of possessions."[32] Indeed, such possessions usually add to the distractions that keep us from an awareness of God's presence, which is the essential ingredient in an identity in God rather than in the world.

This can easily look like an economic and political issue between the haves and the have nots, but Jesus is addressing something much deeper. Jesus is always calling us out of our identity in the world and into an identity in God. Taking economic and political sides can easily miss the point. Our identity is to be in God and not in either wealth or poverty. Compassion for the poor and working on their behalf can be a "works gospel" based upon a worldly identity that leads to a sense of righteousness rather than repentance just as the Protestant Ethic and the Prosperity Gospel can.

This is not to argue that there is a right and wrong notion of Christianity. When we speak of epistemic truth as something to believe, we speak about being right or wrong, but when we speak about ontological truth concerning our being, it is a matter of becoming. We always begin the spiritual journey in the world, but Jesus is always calling us to a deeper life and identity in God rather than in the world. Someone may forgive in order

---

32. Luke 12:15.

to look good to others, or even out of obedience to Jesus words, but that is different from forgiving because you love forgiveness and have made it a part of your identity. Likewise, someone may give without expecting to get anything in return in order increase her worldly identity or even out of obedience to Jesus, but that is different from giving because it has become part of her identity. The spiritual journey to which Jesus calls us may begin with little more than an acceptance of Jesus' forgiveness, but the end of the spiritual journey is always that deeper identity in God.

That deeper identity in God comes by immersing ourselves in Jesus' words and making them our own. We can only do that, however, from that deep place of prayer beneath our identity in the world, since it is only from that place of prayer and who we are in God that we can see how beautiful Jesus' words are. From our identity in the world, it makes no sense to love our enemies, to resist no evil, and to give to all who ask without expecting anything in return. As long as we remain who we are in our worldly identity, we have little choice but to ignore Jesus' teachings and focus exclusively upon his death and resurrection. Some may take it a bit further and force loving behavior upon enemies and give grudgingly to those who ask, but they do so out of obedience rather than being so in love with Jesus' words that we make them our own. Making Jesus' words the basis for our identity is the path of the spiritual journey into a deeper identity in God, but we only begin to move into that deeper identity in God from that core of our existence that is the place of prayer.

Most Christians are quick to confess that Jesus is the son of God. The thing that most Christians have trouble believing is Jesus repeatedly telling us that we are *all* God's daughters and sons. Jesus constantly used the metaphor, "Father" for God, which means that our relationship with God is that of a daughter or son. Twenty-five times throughout the Gospels, Jesus refers to God as "*our* Father," "*your* Father," "*your* heavenly Father," or "*your* Father in heaven."[33] That is hard to believe and dangerous as well. If the only *you* that you know is the person that you and the world have created, the belief that you are God's beloved daughter or son can have devastating consequences. It inflates the ego with false notions of power, wisdom, and pride, but God is not the father and creator of the person that you and the world have created—God is the creator and lover of your soul, which is that pure consciousness at the core of your being. That is the self that God has created and wants to father. For that to happen, however, we need to spend time in the Divine presence at the core of our being as Jesus did.

Repentance or changing our mind is about getting to that deeper level of being, which is the same level of being out of which Jesus spoke. Most of what Jesus has to say is coming out of that deeper level of being that he experiences with the Father in prayer. He repeatedly says that he "can do nothing on his own, but only what he sees the Father doing; for whatever the Father does, the Son does likewise."[34] Because so much of what Jesus has to say is coming out of that deeper level of consciousness that he shares with the Father, it makes little or no sense to us because we

---

33. Matthew 5:16, 45, 48; 6:1, 4, 6, 6, 8, 9, 14, 15, 18, 18, 26, 32; 7:11;10:20, 29; 18:14; Mark 11:25; Luke 6:36; 11:13; 12:30, 32; John 20:17. Note that in Matthew 6:6 and 18 he mentions it twice.

34. John 5:19. Also see, John 5:30 and John 12:49-50.

are seldom at that deepest level of being where there is just you and God and none of the distractions of the world.

From our normal level of being in the world, we are constantly focusing our attention on the distractions that keep us from an awareness of God's presence. T. S. Eliot's great line, "Distracted from distraction by distraction" is a great description of our human condition and our normal state of mind. In fact, this is the only state of mind that many of us know, and when someone tells us of a state of mind where there are no distractions but only our conscious awareness of God's presence, we tend to dismiss their claim since we have never experienced such a state. Indeed, it sounds like heresy when Catherine of Genoa (1447-1510) says, "my deepest me is God." Of course, that was Jesus' experience as well, and the experience of all who are able to descend into prayer beneath all the distractions that occupy and possess our minds.

Prayer, as a matter of getting beneath all the distractions that keep us from an awareness of God's presence, gets us to that perspective from which we can see how divinely beautiful and good Jesus' words are. Without that deeper identity and the perspective it affords, we ignore most of Jesus' teachings. Jesus' prescription that we should love our enemies, give to whoever asks without expecting anything in return, and resist no evil but turn the other cheek when we experience violence[35] seems out of touch with reality, and indeed it is, when seen from the perspective of who we are in the world.

We want Jesus to meet us where we are at, and he does; but he is always calling us to that deeper identity in God. We are very

---

35. Matthew 5:39-44.

content with Jesus as Savior, but few are interested in a Jesus that will change us into a different way to *be*. We want Jesus' truth to be something to believe in but not something to become. We want Jesus to make us righteous but we want him to make us into *our* idea of righteousness rather than *his* idea of righteousness. This is why we prefer other portions of scripture to build our lives around. We love those parts of the Bible that depict the early stages of the spiritual journey but not the words of Jesus, which show us the end of the spiritual journey to which we are being called.

The Bible, however, is not only true but it is realistic as well. It depicts people in relationship with God from a variety of perspectives, just as we in our own spiritual journeys have experienced and interpreted our God experiences from a variety of perspectives that represent our understanding at different points in the journey. We always begin with a wrong understanding of God. Our initial understanding is usually a god that represents who *we* would be if we were God. It is God as seen from our perspective in the world, but Jesus is calling us to a different perspective. Indeed, he is calling us to his own perspective, which reflects our identity in God.

The god we begin with rewards and punishes whatever our tribe or culture says is good or evil. Jesus never quotes or references those portions of scripture. He never quotes from books like Numbers, Joshua, or Judges. He came to fulfill the law because he understood that the purpose of the law was to bring us to repentance and not to make us appear righteous. Much of what appears in the Old Testament is about people trying to appear righteous before God in order to gain God's favor. That was never God's purpose and this is why we have to read the Old Testament scripture through Jesus rather than reading Jesus in the context of the entire Bible. Jesus is the filter, and those portions of scripture that match up with the things that Jesus says represent the God of which Jesus speaks, rather than the god that our particular tribes create in their likeness.

We usually begin with a god that is the most that we can imagine from the perspective of who we are in the world. That is why we ignore so much of what Jesus says. The Bible is God's beautiful revelation of human beings seeking God but all too quickly believing that they know God and what God desires, when in fact, they are at very early parts of the journey to which God calls us. The mystery of God is much greater than we imagine. Eventually, however, the author of the story enters into the story itself not to explain the mystery of God but to show us how to experience and *be* in the midst of that mystery that is God.

As we have said, God never had to get rid of our sins in order to love us. That is in our head and it is where we usually begin in our understanding of God based upon our experience with human authority. That is where God initially meets us but God is constantly calling us to something deeper. God allowed the Jewish people to have kings, even though it was not God's idea,[36] and he allowed them to have divorce,[37] even though it was not his idea. He also allowed them to have blood sacrifices in order to feel worthy enough to approach their idea of a holy God. Furthermore, Jesus was even willing to be the blood sacrifice for those whose idea of God required a blood sacrifice, but God never needed a blood sacrifice in order to love us. God loves us in the midst of our sin, and Jesus is trying to teach us how to love

---

36. 1 Samuel 8:1-22.
37. Matthew 19:8.

others in the midst of whatever we happen to think their sins are. This is the nature of the spiritual journey, but we can only go as far in the journey as our identity allows. People with tribal identities could never hear from a God who told them to love their enemies and not respond to violence with violence. In order to hear from such a God, one's identity must be *in God* rather than *in the tribe.* Someone whose identity is that of a businessperson cannot hear a God that tells us to give without expecting anything in return. In order to hear from such a God one needs to find a different identity in God rather than an identity as a businessperson. Most Christians ignore the hard things that Jesus says because we can only hear those things when our identity is in God rather than the world. This is why transformation is so essential to the Christian life. The transformation, however, is not from sinner to saint because our behavior or beliefs have changed. It is much deeper than that. What changes with our transformation or sanctification is that our identity is no longer in the world, but in God, just as Jesus' identity was in God rather than in the world.

What many Christians understand by religious conversion or the born again experience is that Jesus has saved them from going to hell and they are now going to heaven because of what Jesus has done on the cross, but that is just the beginning of the story. Jesus intends our heavenly existence to begin *now* and not at some point after our physical death. Of course, in order for us to begin our heavenly existence now, we need to change our identity from being in the world to being in God. This is what underlies all of Jesus' teachings and why people who are in the world ignore those teachings. He is trying to give us his perspective of what it means to have our identity in God rather than in the world. This presents a problem for people who want to enter God's kingdom—but not now. They like their identity in the world and do not want it to end in order to come into a new identity in God until they lose their identity in the world with their physical death. They hate the fact that Jesus tells us that we need to give up all of our possessions and follow him into a new way to be *in* God rather than *in* the world. This is the deeper repentance to which Jesus is always calling us, but it is hardest to hear for those whose identity in the world is great. They are much more attracted to theologies that tell them they can have Jesus and the world as well. All they have to do is ignore the words of Jesus and build their faith around other portions of scripture that reflect a more human perspective rather than the divine perspective to which Jesus calls us.

The words of Jesus are always calling us to a deeper level of being *in* God. Such a journey, however, involves the death of who we are in the world in order that our new life in God might come forth. Jesus says, "For those who want to save their life will lose it, and those who lose their life for my sake will find it."[38] We are in a constant need of death and resurrection in order to come into the fullness of life to which Jesus calls us. What keeps us from that fullness of life is the belief that we already have it and we are at the end of the journey: Jesus has saved us from our sin—end of story.

We want to believe that there is no spiritual journey and that the Christian life is simply about getting our sins forgiven so we can spend eternity in heaven, rather than following Jesus into the fullness of life to which he calls us. We do not want to believe

---

38. Matthew 16:25.

that these two Christians narratives are simply different places in the same spiritual journey, and that Jesus is always calling us to an ever-deeper intimacy with both God and ourselves. The great temptation that we always face is to call an end to the spiritual journey and see our identity in the world as God's blessing. In order to do so, however, we have to avoid the words of Jesus, which are the eternal anomalies to whatever theologies we construct and attach what we call our faith. The journey to which Jesus' words "Follow me"[39] call us may begin with repentance for behavioral sins, but God's purpose for our lives is much more than overcoming disobedience to divine commandments. God's ultimate purpose is to make us into Jesus likeness, but for that to happen there can be no end to our need for repentance for not spending more time in the Divine presence and Jesus' words.

---

39. Matthew 4:19; 8:22; 9:9; 16:24; 19:21; Mark 2:14; 8:34; 10:21; Luke 5:27; 9:23, 59; 18:22; John 1:43; 10:27; 12:26; 13:36; 21:19.

CHAPTER NINE

Kept from the Journey

THE SPIRITUAL JOURNEY to which Jesus calls us is one of becoming ever more like Jesus. The way that happens is by seeing how beautiful and good his words are and making those words the basis for our identity. Three things keep us from that journey. The first is our concept of truth, which comes from the Greeks and Aristotle in particular rather than Jesus. Recall that Aristotle's concept of truth was simply something to know rather than something to be which would include the good and the beautiful as well as what is true. Epistemic truth, which is merely something to know, requires theories or conceptual paradigms that have to change over time in order to accommodate our ever-expanding experience that presents anomalies to our understanding. The microscope and the world it uncovered made Aristotle's understanding of the world obsolete, just as Einstein's world made Newton's mechanical understanding obsolete. Today, dark matter and dark energy are the latest anomalies to confound our theoretical understanding. Based upon what we know from our twenty-first century perspective, there is no reason to suppose that at some point in the future all the data will be in and all future anomalies eliminated. From our twenty-first century perspective, the world seems to be forever beyond our understanding, and if Creation is beyond our understanding how much more is its Creator.

Theologies that purport to encapsulate the Creator within an epistemic truth that we can possess are naive at best. The words of Jesus are always calling us to something beyond epistemic truth. They are words that confound our understanding and instead direct us toward a way to *be*.

> Everyone then who hears these words of mine and acts on them will be like a wise man who built his house on rock. The rain fell, the floods came, and the wind blew and beat on that house, but it did not fall, because it had been founded on rock. And everyone who hears these words of mine and does not act upon them will be like the foolish man who built his house on sand. The rain fell, and the floods came, and the winds blew and beat against the house, and it fell—and great was its fall![1]

The truth to which Jesus calls us is not a theoretical truth concerning our knowledge of God and ourselves. Although the spiritual journey may begin with such a truncated notion of truth, the words of Jesus always call us to something deeper that involves our very being rather than simply our knowing. Knowing Jesus' words is more like knowing how to do something rather than knowing answers to questions in order to give us the pseudo sense of security that comes from our pretense to knowledge. The ontological truth to which Jesus calls us is not a theoretical knowing but a knowing how to be like Jesus. Knowing Jesus is a matter of knowing how to forgive—knowing how to be merciful. That is

---

1. Matthew 7:24-27.

the knowing to which he calls us. Do you know how to find your way to that secret place of prayer where only you and God can go? Jesus knew how to do that, and that is the kind of knowing to which he is calling us. Are you good at finding that place on a regular basis so you can be aware of the Divine presence as Jesus was? This is the knowing, which comes from building your life upon the rock of which Jesus speaks.

When Jesus says, "I am the way, and the truth, and the life,"[2] he is speaking of a way to *be* that draws its truth, life, and identity from a particular kind of relationship with God. Jesus' original followers departed from the common beliefs of their day in order to follow Jesus into a new way to *be* in God rather than in the world. To have your identity in God rather than in the world is very different from believing in epistemic truths. While our eternal relationship to God is certainly established and maintained through the kind of forgiveness and mercy that Jesus reveals from the cross, the fullness of life to which Jesus calls us does not come by simply believing that as a factual truth. That may be where we begin, but the fullness of life to which Jesus calls us only comes through a process of falling evermore in love with the words of Jesus and making them the basis of our identity. In order to do that, however, we have to stop identifying with who we are in the world, and come to a new identity in God.

Christianity has not had much of an effect upon the world because the more popular Christian narrative is one that sells righteousness in exchange for mere epistemic belief. The less popular but more effective narrative is one of nearly perpetual repentance

---

2. John 14:6.

for not making Jesus' words our own, and therein coming to know how to be forgiving and merciful for having received much forgiveness and mercy, rather than making a pretense to righteousness because of what we claim to believe. Of course, the popular gospel will claim that what we are suggesting is a works gospel rather than a faith gospel, but it is not a matter of *works* but a matter of *identity*. Do we identify with the words of Jesus or the world?

The words of Jesus are not commandments to obey but a picture of who Jesus is calling us to be. They are words that reveal the spiritual journey to which we aspire. They are words that reveal the true way that God desires human beings to be. In order for us to pursue such a truth, we need to recognize truth as something to *be* rather than something merely to know. Truth as something to know can never get us beyond obedience. To get us to fall in love with Jesus, we need to see how divinely beautiful and supremely good his words are. Unfortunately, that is not something that we can see from the perspective of who we are in the world. From our worldly perspective, we do not think that it is beautiful and good that God is "kind to the ungrateful and the wicked."[3] From the perspective of who we are in the world, we believe it is good to hate our enemies and to respond to evil with violence. We can only see the beauty and goodness of Jesus' words from that deeper level of being "in God" rather than in the world. That is why, although the "born again" experience begins with a profession of what we believe, the spiritual journey that follows is about our ceasing to identify with the world and coming to identify with who we are in God.

---

3. Luke 6:35.

Having an identity in the world rather than an identity in God is the second thing, in addition to our concept of truth, that keeps us from the fullness of life to which Jesus calls us. We think there is nothing wrong with identifying with who we are in the world, but Jesus' words are all about bringing us to repentance for identifying with who we are in the world rather than who we are in God. That is not something that we can see from early places in the spiritual journey, however. We begin the spiritual journey from the perspective of who we are in the world, but Jesus' words always call us to that new perspective of who we are in God. An identity in God is the end of a spiritual journey of repentance for not falling evermore in love with Jesus' words and making them the foundation of our being. Jesus' words always call us to repentance rather than righteousness. Religious people claim to righteousness because of what they believe. This is what Jesus called hypocrisy in his day, and that has not changed. Jesus is not calling us to a new set of *beliefs* but a new way to *be*. Of course, it may begin with a new set of beliefs but it always moves toward a new identity in God rather than the world.

Jesus' words are neither wise nor helpful instructions on how to conform and prosper in the world. They are words that are wise and useful, however, for those who wish to conform to a world that has never been but is the world toward which God's spirit continues to draw us. The idea of living for a world that has never been is not something that most people find appealing. Most Christians want to know how God wants them to live in this world, and for that, they look to the Bible, but Jesus is telling us how to live in a heavenly world to come. We interpret that as a world to come after our death, but the world of which Jesus speaks is also the world that fuels human evolution and history. Jesus is not only the Alpha of history and the reason it all began with the big bang, but he is also the Omega toward which all of history is evolving. Jesus is the perfect human being made in God's likeness and the prototype for God's creation. In order to see that, however, we not only need a more divine concept of truth than the one that Aristotle had provided, but we need a new identity in God rather than the identity we have created for ourselves in the world. In order to develop such an identity in God based upon Jesus' concept of truth as something to *be,* we need to pray.

Prayer is the third essential element necessary for the transformative journey into Jesus' likeness, but it is not prayer, as we initially understand that concept. We begin the spiritual journey from the perspective of who we are in the world, so it is natural that our prayers are a matter of petitioning God regarding our worldly circumstances, but Jesus' words are always calling us to that deeper life in God rather than the life we have created for ourselves in the world. We only become aware of that deeper life, however, as we spend time in God's presence beneath all the concerns and desires that arise from our being in the world. The place of prayer to which Jesus calls us is that place where we desire nothing more than an awareness of God's presence. What keeps us from that place is that we are constantly in the world, and its concerns possess us and keep us from an awareness of the Divine presence that Jesus knew so well. As we have said, prayer is that place deep within our soul where only you and God can go; it is that place you go to in order to be alone with God. We all have such a place at the core of our being but the concerns of the world that constantly demand our attention keep us from an awareness of that place.

Unfortunately, many Christians are oblivious of such a place of prayer and the kind of repentance or change of mind that it takes to get to that deeper place where we are *in God* rather than *in the world*. Most Christians pray from the perspective of who they are in the world, but are unaware of that deeper level of being to which Jesus is constantly calling us. They are thankful Christians but they have no place in their lives for the kind of repentance that would lead them to that deeper place of being in God rather than being in the world. They see themselves as righteous because of their religious beliefs and practices and therefore no longer in need of repentance. Jesus tells a story about such people. He says that two men went up to the temple to pray one was a Pharisee and the other a tax collector.

> The Pharisee, standing by himself, was praying thus, "God, I thank you that I am not like other men: thieves, rogues, adulterers, or even like this tax collector. I fast twice a week; I give a tenth of all my income." But the tax collector, standing far off, would not even look up to heaven, but was beating his breast and saying, "God, be merciful to me, a sinner!" I tell you, that this man went down to his home justified rather than the other; for all that exalt themselves will be humbled, but all who humble themselves will be exalted.[4]

The spiritual journey to which Jesus calls us begins and ends with repentance. Jesus' first teaching, which immediately precedes the Sermon on the Mount in the first of the four Gospels, is, "Repent, for the Kingdom of heaven has come near."[5] The

---

4. Luke 18:10-14.
5. Matthew 4:17.

popular forms of Christianity have interpreted repentance as a call to stop doing bad things, start doing good things, and profess a belief in Jesus as Savior. The popular form of Christianity sees this repentance as a single event, which transforms us from being under God's wrath to being the object of God's love, but the repentance to which Jesus calls us is the perpetual means by which we go from being in the world to being in God. Repentance (*metanoia*) is the changing of our mind from being in the world to a radically different way to be *in* God.

In the world, it is easy to imagine ourselves as righteous, because in the world we compare ourselves to other human beings who are guilty of sins of which we are innocent. Today, as in Jesus' day, it is popular for righteous, religious people to point out the sins of others for which they themselves are not guilty. Today, it is popular for religious, heterosexual males to point out the sins of abortion and homosexuality. How can they not see the hypocrisy in that? Imagining that the greatest sins are ones that you can never be guilty of is hypocrisy in its most diabolical form.

Of course, as long as our identity remains in the world rather than in God, we cannot imagine God desiring anything more from us than obedience. Righteousness as obedience is as far as who we are in the world can go. Falling in love with Jesus in order to become like the Divine in terms of mercy and forgiveness is beyond the reach of our worldly identity. Transformation into his likeness requires a different kind of being and we only discover that deeper way to be as we spend time in God's presence from the core of our being. Jesus would often go off to solitary places to pray,[6] and in order for his words to bring us to the deeper life to which he calls us, we need to seek that solitude and silence of prayer as well.

As we have seen, attention is the essential ingredient of love. It is what we desire from others and what God desires from us. The way we come to know other human beings is by spending time with them and giving them our undivided attention, and it is no different with God. This is the ultimate nature of prayer and what determines the kind of love we have for God. At the beginning of the spiritual journey, God is like the enormously wealthy grandfather who we visit whenever we need something, rather than for the pleasure of his company. From our perspective in the world that is the best that we can do since from that perspective we interpret everything through the filter of self-interest, but there is a deeper place within us where those filters no longer exist and we simply enjoy the pleasure of being in the presence of God. It is the raw experience of our connection to the Divine and the pleasure of that experience. When we are in that place, our identity is in God and not the world, and from that place we can see the beauty and goodness of Jesus' words.

When we begin to identify with who we are in the silence of God's presence at the core of our being, we are in the very place from which Jesus communed with the Father and it is only from that place that we begin to resonate with the beauty and wisdom of Jesus' words. As long as we remain in the world, the words of Jesus will always baffle us and we will find ways around them. The most popular way around the words of Jesus is to understand

6. Matthew 14:23, 26:36; Mark 1:35, 6:46; Luke 5:16, 6:12.

them in the context of the rest of the Bible, so when Jesus tells us to love our enemies, we find other places in the Bible where God tells us to kill our enemies. When Jesus tells us that wealth is sinful, we find other places in the Bible where wealth seems to be a blessing from God. This leaves us with a capricious God, but equally, the freedom to decide whether this is a time for killing our enemies or loving them. It gives us the freedom to decide whether virtue lies in our wealth or our poverty.

The other option is to read the Bible in the context of the Jesus revelation; that is, that Jesus gets it right and is the end of the spiritual journey to which God calls us. Jesus tells us "the gate is narrow and the road is hard that leads to life, and there are few who find it."[7] He does not tell us where the gate is or how to find it, however, because he is the gate and the hard road. He simply says, "Follow me."[8] These are the only directions given by Jesus, so we look to other places in scripture from which to construct easier paths than the one Jesus calls us to follow. We argue that he was God and therefore his path is not one that we could successfully follow. The beauty of the Gospel, however, lies in the fact that as we set Jesus' teachings before us, we see an almost constant need for repentance and the consequent experience of God's mercy and forgiveness for our failure to be as Jesus calls us to be. Of course, being aware of the fact that we are the constant recipients of God's mercy and forgiveness is the very thing that does transform us into his merciful and forgiving likeness, since

---

7. Matthew 7:14.

8. Matthew 4:19; 8:22; 9:9; 16:24; 19:21; Mark 2:14; 8:34; 10:21; Luke 5:27; 9:23, 59; 18:22; John 1:43; 10:27; 12:26; 13:36; 21:19.

"the one to whom little is forgiven, loves little."[9]

In order to experience such great amounts of mercy and forgiveness in order that we might love much, we have to see that our real sin is not our disobedience to God's law concerning our behavior but that our identity and life is in the world and not in God. Transformation into the Divine likeness is the end of the spiritual journey but that transformation only takes place as we come to identify with who we are in God in the deep silence of our soul. As long as we avoid that deep place of prayer, our relationship with God will always be superficial and based upon who we are in the world rather than our identity in God. As long as our identity is in the world rather than in God, we will put our faith in what we claim to know, but as we have seen, our pretense to knowledge always encounters anomalies that confound what we claim to know. Our only true security comes, not from what we claim to know, but from the intimate experience of the mystery of God's presence in the deepest recesses of our being. This place of prayer at the core of our being is a place from which we are no longer confident in our own understanding but the mystery has taken hold of us and we draw our confidence from that hold it has upon us. The more familiar we become with who we are in that great silence of prayer, the less likely we will be to interpret our prayerful experiences through the prejudices of our socio-cultural understanding. The more time we spend in the silence of God's presence, the freer we become to explore the fullness of God unfettered by those parochial and provincial notions that keep us from seeing the beauty and wisdom of Jesus' words.

---

9. Luke 7:47.

Prayer is the place of fasting from the world and all of the world's concerns in order to discover our soul and its connection to the Divine. The more we visit that place and come to identify with it rather than the world, the more we become that pure perceiver who has taken on the Jesus perspective. From that place of the raw experience of God's presence, we are able to have faith in God rather than faith in our religious tradition and beliefs. If we are unfamiliar with that deeper level of prayer, and instead, identify with who we are in the world, we will all too quickly interpret our experiences with God through our own understanding, which always thinks that its science and theology are the last word and capable of reducing the mystery to a puzzle that we have solved.

People who attempt to get their security needs met by either religion or science consider it heresy to depart from the conventional understanding of their day. The conventional wisdom of both science and religion, however, changes with the vicissitudes of history in order to accommodate the anomalies we inevitably encounter. Trusting in the popular theology of a particular time and place is comforting because many people endorse that popular perspective, but it always represents something less than the fullness of life to which prayer and Jesus' words constantly call us. The silence and solitude of prayer, along with the words of Jesus, provide the perennial path to that eternal and ineffable truth that does not vary over time or from one culture to another. This is the narrow gate and hard road that Jesus says leads to life.[10] Jesus tells us to build our lives upon the rock, which he tells us are his

---

10. "For the gate is narrow and the road is hard that leads to life and there are few who find it." Matthew 7:14.

words,[11] but those words have little meaning to us without a deep repentance for being in the world and living out of the mind the world has given us rather than the mind of Christ that Jesus' words provide.

The great blessing of our day is that history has exposed the fact that epistemic truth is always local and relative to a particular time, place, and language. The spiritual journey may begin with epistemic beliefs concerning what we know and believe but it always moves toward the deeper ontological truth of having our identity and being in God rather than in the world. Jesus' truth is not something to know because it is true but something to be because it is divinely beautiful and good. Truth is a matter of being rather than knowing and Jesus is the ultimate form of that truth to which he calls us.

There is nothing new in this. This is what the great saints have always known; that is, that Jesus' truth was not something to simply know and believe but something to become. Jesus knew who he was in God and who we are in God at the core of our being. His words are constantly instructing us concerning our identity in God rather than the lie of who we are in the world. Of course, that is not where we begin. We start in the world and seek a little bit of God to help us with our existence in the world. God, however, is always calling us back to that original state of deep communion with God before the world got a hold of us and begins making us into its likeness rather than the Divine likeness. This is the deep story that underlies the Bible and all of human history.

---

11. Matthew 7:24-27.

Interestingly, one of the consequences of realizing that Jesus' truth is something to be rather than simply something to know and believe is that it provides the only path for realizing Jesus' prayer that his followers would be one as he and the Father are one. In the seventeenth chapter of John's Gospel, Jesus prays, "As you, Father, are in me and I am in you, may they also be in us, so that the world may believe that you have sent me. The glory that you have given me I have given to them, so that they may be one, as we are one."[12]

Christians who believe that Jesus' truth is merely an epistemic truth that is no more than something to know and believe will never realize that prayer of Jesus. Epistemic truths change with the vicissitudes that influence language and theories. The words of Jesus, however, point us toward an eternal way to *be* that is always beyond us, so no one can boast. The more we pursue the kind of being to which Jesus calls us, the more we are humbled, brought to repentance, and continue to bask in the divine mercy and forgiveness that transforms us into his likeness.

Our theologies and doctrines divide us into tens of thousands of Christian denominations, many believing that they alone have the precise words and theologies to unlock the mysteries of God. When, however, we see Jesus as the truth and our lives as pursuing that way of being, we find that our common failure and perpetual repentance unites us in a mercy and forgiveness that is far more real than our theologies. Our theologies and doctrines only divide and increase our identity in the world as we compare ourselves to one another rather than to Jesus. What unites us into the common

---

12. John 17:21-22.

oneness for which Jesus prays is our common failure to be as he calls us to be.